Wisdom for the Aging

Wisdom for the Aging

*Practical Advice for Living the Best Years of
Your Life Right Now*

By

Malcolm Boyd

LeaderResources

Leeds, Massachusetts

Library of Congress Control Number: 2009926648

Published by LeaderResources
P.O. Box 302, Leeds, MA 01053

ISBN: 978-1-59518-043-8

www.LeaderResources.org

To Mark Thompson

Wisdom for the Aging

∾ Contents ∾

∾ Preface ∾

When did I become aware that I was aging?

It might have been my thirtieth birthday. Thirty seemed so old then. I remember asking is there life after thirty? If one hadn't made a million dollars yet, was there any point to continue trying?

A couple of decades later, fifty terrified me. I guess it was that half-century reference. Damn, that sounded old. I drove to a nearby pharmacy and checked out hair dyes. Black! That's what I needed to get rid of the gray. Coming back home, I stood before the mirror and applied it. What I saw was a disaster to rival the Titanic. I hadn't achieved my intention to be transformed into the breathtakingly handsome Clark Gable of "Gone With the Wind." Chastened, I washed out the dye. A Hamlet mood settled inside me. Reaching for a soliloquy, I pondered deep meanings of self. This clearly meant, however, making a decision to be myself.

Some years later I stood in line at a movie boxoffice to buy a ticket. The cashier surprised me by asking "Don't you want a senior discount?" I was stunned and embarrassed. All I wanted was a ticket, not a reminder (in public) that apparently

I looked older. Had I, in fact, changed into an aging person? What could that possibly mean?

I remember another movie boxoffice some years afterward. I was seventy. Standing in line, I grasped my wallet to pay. Looking at the cashier, I said "Senior, please." She gave me a hard look. In an instant old tables had changed. An odd situation had completely reversed itself. "I need an identification," she said. "Do you have a driver's license?"

By now aging was cropping up all over the place as a puzzling fact of my life. For example, my doctor ordered an x-ray to determine if there was osteoarthritis in my back. Cataract surgery suddenly loomed ahead. Then my genial dentist remarked offhandedly that apparently I was grinding my teeth during sleep time and would need fillings.

Yet aging, I soon discovered, was so much more than all these things. Death itself was drawing closer. (I'd be checking out. What would that be like?) How would I be able to handle the pragmatic details of the dying process? At a deeper level I asked: what had I made of life? Had I loved other people enough? Learned how to forgive? Given more than I had taken? Understood friendship? Done something to change the world for the better, maybe just in my own metaphorical backyard?

At eighty-five, I find aging is a remarkable opportunity. To make changes in my own life and life around me. Become more flexible, open to change, learning how to be an enabler of it. Honor memory while managing to look ahead, not behind.

Let the present moment into my consciousness. I like these words novelist Julie Glass wrote in her book *I See You Everywhere*: "When was the last time anything seemed AMAZING to me?"

As an Episcopal priest and spiritual director for more than fifty years, I've worked with elders and their families in countless situations. As a writer, I've watched as aging has become a principal part of my life. Around twenty years ago my writing career enabled me to enter into an experience of unusual insight. To my utter surprise I was invited to write a regular column on aging for the thirty-four million readers of the *AARP Magazine* (then called *Modern Maturity*).

My assignment embraced a decade. My format took the form of responses to questions from my readers. Every sort of question came my way. Here are a few of the many.

"I find that the habit of despair is a bottomless pit. I wonder if I can achieve the habit of hope instead?"

"I try hard to be happy. I work at it. But I'm not happy. What is the secret of being happy?"

"Why can't a child return to a parent even a bit of the love that has been poured out unselfishly and at vast sacrifice?"

"I realize I am not going to live forever. Can I handle this?"

"I often wonder why we elderly folk are so stubborn and self-centered. Why can't we love our kids enough to give up our own desires and make it easier for all?"

"How can I deal honestly with life as it is, not as I wish it were?"

"My ritual of sameness, day after day, makes me feel simply numb. Can I change?"

"My husband died eight months ago. I can't accept the fact that he's not coming back. I can't live without him. He was everything to me. I cry all the time. I cry when I go to bed and reach out and there is only a pillow there."

"My lover and I broke up four years ago and I've been living alone. I'm a sixty-seven-year old lesbian and a successful businesswoman who has a workaholic streak. Recently I met another woman who loves me and has asked to make a life with me. But I'm afraid. I don't know if I dare risk a new relationship."

Over the years as I responded to readers of my AARP column on aging these women and men tellingly became real people to me. I was moved when they trusted me with their life stories, feelings, emotions, fears and hopes. The sheer diversity of the letters I received was astonishing. I especially liked warm, intimate storytelling ones, chock-full of details, that mysteriously connected dots.

The best wisdom for the aging that I've accumulated, however, has been gleaned from my own life. As a Manhattan kid caught in the divorce of my parents and transported to Colorado in the midst of the Great Depression in 1930, my own wisdom was forever linked to the inevitability of change.

Early I learned that living requires courage and hard discipline, the deepest possible commitment and the presence of helpful companions. A passion for life has always been a part of my approach to it. Always I sought role models.

One close at hand was my mother Beatrice. She worked hard most of her life. She found joy in everyday things like painting, caring for her beloved dogs, and tending her garden. Upon retirement, she became a volunteer teacher at the Childrens Hospital of Los Angeles. She washed and pressed her uniform and for years drove into the hospital to perform her duties. One day a young boy asked "You're old, aren't you?" Beatrice replied yes. "Good," he said, "then I can talk to you."

After she fell and broke her hip, Mother lived in a nursing facility for several years until her death at ninety-nine. Her death was simple and natural. I was with her at the end. It reminded me of psychotherapist Irvin D. Yalom's words in his book *Love's Executioner*: "I have always felt that the way one faces death is greatly determined by the model one's parents set."

During Beatrice's long stay in a nursing home preceding her death, I had become—among other things—a son caring for an elderly parent. So I learned painstakingly the precise rhythms of a convalescent hospital or nursing facility: its smells, rules, philosophies, cast of characters, points of strength and beauty, and finally the sheer patience required to survive.

Aging, I found, requires learning. God knows it requires wisdom. It can be an enormous blessing because it serves to sum up a life, lend it character, underscore its motivation. Finally, it prepares the way for leavetaking.

∽ Relationships ∽

"My mother is in her late sixties and is becoming a recluse. She refuses to make any sense out of her life, neglects her health, won't learn a skill or work, is running out of money rapidly, and it's driving me crazy. I can't communicate with her because we always end up shouting at each other over the phone. It would be a lot easier if she were dead."

~

It seems that one of the hardest lessons to learn is that we are unable to live another person's life. Parents often try with grim determination to live their children's lives: "You *will* do what I say." "I'm going to teach you how to do this if I have to break your neck."

Ironically, children sometimes try to do the same thing with older parents, reversing roles: "*I* know what is best for you." "*Why* don't you behave the way I want you to do?" But the meaning of love includes letting go. A person has the right to his or her own life, without our interference. The closer we are to someone, the more we can try to act like a dictator. Better to be a friend than a dictator.

Today, I give up control of others' lives. I'll do my best with my own.

"I am HIV-positive and have the AIDS virus. I have been with my lover for eight years and we plan a church blessing of our union. My lover's dad and mom have accepted our invitation to come to the service. My sister will attend, but my father refuses to come. This means my mom won't be there either. It makes me sad to see my family split like this."

~

We have to make decisions in our life that are not dependent on the feelings and wishes of others, no matter how close they may be.

When we decide what we're going to go, we've really announced that we are self-reliant, know our mind, have set our course, and are not waiting for a U.N. resolution to provide us with a mandate.

After we make our decision, it's up to others to react as they wish. We should be ready for a variety of responses, ranging from negative to positive ones. It's important to respect the feelings of others and try to understand them. A helpful way to do this is to try looking at our situation through their eyes. However, this does not in any way affect our decision. It's been made.

I'll expect the best response from others. I'll be grateful when I'm right. But I'll do what I know is right regardless.

"My husband is having an affair at seventy-two. He was indiscreet enough to take her out to dinner at a restaurant where a friend of mine ran into them. My friend called me first thing the next morning to tell me about it. My husband is a doddering old fool and I could wring his neck."

~

There are reasons why people do things. It's important for us to know the reasons as well as the things.

Sometimes we share in the responsibility, even though we don't want to admit it. We may not even grasp it. Yet this doesn't save us from participating in the consequences.

If someone else does something that hurts us, part of the responsibility is to bring it out into the open with that person. Not sweep it under a rug. Not pretend it isn't there. Not wish it would go away. And a sense of humor may be the most essential ingredient in a situation laced with misunderstanding and bitterness. After all, the human comedy has the longest run of all.

Today, I'll face the truth. I'll try to see the humor as well as the sadness of it.

"Three old people live in a house three houses up the street from mine. They are one man and two women. I understand the man is married to one of the women, and the other is her sister. They are quiet as church mice, secretive, never mix with the neighbors, and this disturbs me."

~

Secretly in some inner chamber of the heart, we seem to yearn for everybody to be the same. Is this a reason why diversity so often troubles and threatens us?

People are different. When our own differentness is called into question, we appreciate it when *our* individuality is respected. We have our own tastes, ideas, and feelings. We don't wish to be destroyed in an impersonal melting pot.

Neither do most other people. Some people want to be alone, others desire to be out in a crowd. Some cherish ethnic, religious, cultural tokens of diversity that become personal symbols of identity. There is plenty of room for both. Instead of being disturbed by obvious manifestations of diversity, we should be grateful for our own freedom, and support the freedom of others.

How has conformity kept me from my own path? I'll respect difference where I find it, in myself, and in others.

"The son or daughter who takes on the responsibility of caring for an elderly parent is never prepared to deal with the guilt that caring leaves behind."

~

Caring for anyone is a sensitive and complicated thing to do. It requires endless patience, self-control, and an awareness of someone else's feelings.

There can be drudgery involved in caring. One person is ostensibly in a position of control while the other is not. This can lead to resistance against authority on the one hand, and misuse of power on the other.

Anger can easily come to the forefront in such a relationship, along with frustration, emotional fatigue, and cruelty. The person who is caring must realize that the other is dependant, needy, and not always in command of his or her resources. This is an uneven coupling of people possessing vastly different strengths, weaknesses, and skills. Guilt can follow when we lose patience and give way to emotions that ravage our spirit and hurt the other.

Today, I'll stop and acknowledge the good I'm doing. I'm grateful for my power to do it.

"I am twelve and live with my grandmother. She drives me crazy. She wants me to act like a lady all the time and just doesn't want to accept the fact that I am not a little girl anymore."

~

Oh, dear. Somebody needs to let Grandma know.

When it comes to age differences, most of us frequently seem to be driving the rest of us crazy. Why doesn't our grandmother act like a grandmother (and quit embarrassing us?) instead of spinning corny stories and staying up late? Why doesn't our granddaughter act like a granddaughter should—be proper, respectful, and well, a lady?

The problem is this: we're human. We're individuals. We don't want anyone building fences around us, constricting our impulses, holding us in, saying No, repressing our energy. We adamantly refuse to let anyone prescribe "correct" behavior for us that feels like a straitjacket. No! We don't want our growth (at whatever age) to be stunted. We won't be forced into a double standard that makes us act this way while our real self is going that way.

It can't be done too often: today, I assert my freedom to simply be myself.

"When I see an elderly bag lady I think: How did she live a whole lifetime and end up alone and without help? It makes me count my friends."

~

One of the most startling sights on a city street is that of an older woman dressed in rags, with a cart that contains all her possessions, lying on a bus stop bench and covered with yesterday's newspapers for warmth. She needs food, clothing, medical care, friends and love. What hideous set of circumstances brought her to such a naked moment of decline and need? We cannot discount her as an aberration or some kind of outsider.

Many stand in peril of occupying her shoes someday. Her condition underscores a denial of compassion and a terrible wrong at the core of our society. This older woman lives alone as an alien on our streets. Poor and defenseless, she is part of our life. She warns us not to let our hearts become hearts of stone.

Today, I'll count the blessings of friendship and support. I'll extend myself to someone lacking these.

"I'm eighty and I go to the Senior Center several times a week, take care of my two great grandchildren one day, and deliver Meals on Wheels. These things get me out and I am with people."

∾

We need to get out and be with other people as much as possible. It's stimulating: we can share and laugh and get new ideas.

Meeting friends at a Senior Center, and maybe volunteering to do some work there, is a splendid idea. It's important to see how others are managing with the same sort of needs and problems that we have. There can be an exchange of everything from self-help remedies to suggestions for pen pals.

Staying alone prevents us from receiving needed input from others. We think too much about ourselves, become fixated on problems, and narrow our focus on life. It's necessary to get our mind off what worries us, and onto how other people are feeling, coping, and what is the dynamic that keeps them going.

I won't try to make it alone. Today, I'll give in to my need for other people.

"My mother hates my wife. She is making it almost impossible for me to be a good son because she keeps insulting my wife and trying to drive a wedge between us. The tension is unbearable."

≈

Some human situations seem more insoluble than others. We find that we're trapped between a rock and a hard place. Nothing gives at all. We search in vain for any answer, let alone an easy one.

While there may not be a single answer, there can be alternative ways to approach our problem. We need to examine these and make choices. For example, given a crisis between two people in our life, we can come to each of them alone and attempt to have a rational discussion about what's wrong, and why. After that, perhaps we need to bring together the two people who are engaged in a crisis. We can ascertain if either one wishes to be isolated with bitterness. If not, it's necessary to find a way to make peace, even a fragile and temporary one.

Today, I'll end an old tension. I won't choose between two unacceptables. I'll make a new one.

"When I visit shut-ins, I put a clown's makeup on my face and wear a clown's costume. To feel the love of new friends is a wonderful experience for both."

~

To bring joy into someone's life is a lovely thing to do. It can take so little effort and reap great rewards.

We should use our imagination when we visit people who are confined to their home or a hospital. Remember, they can't get outside. They need a spiritual light, a ray of sunshine, a bright intrusion into what may otherwise be a drab, plodding, uneventful day. This provides us an opportunity to offer something unusual.

Above all, we shouldn't bring our own problems with us. Leave them at the door. This is a moment to be outgoing, happy, uplifting, magical, energized, and to make someone else feel good. After we leave, hopefully our presence in the room will remain as a sign of lightness, joy, and hope.

I'll play Peter Pan in someone's life and carry a moment of light.

"As an older woman and a widow, I watch those couples who need no one but themselves and I wonder, who's more selfish?"

∼

We're all so different from one another. It's amazing. Some of us are outgoing and gregarious, others shy and reclusive. It's never easy at all to understand someone who represents the other side of the coin.

I wonder why we don't help one another more in understanding each other. We can make it very difficult. Some of us hide our selfishness under the guise of being either outgoing or reclusive. The latter is more easily associated with selfishness because it looks like it. So a withdrawn, loner type of person is usually more easily targeted as being uncaring.

However, a far more sophisticated kind of selfishness may lurk beneath an appearance of gregariousness. Here, an uncaring person can ironically come across as a carbon copy of Mother Theresa. We need to look beneath labels, especially self-manufactured ones.

I'm going to try not to judge. I'm going to live generously, and look for caring and generosity in others.

"I am sixty-six years old and had a constant loving companion for thirty-four years. Since her death, sometimes I think I just can't go on."

~

The loss of a loved one can be terribly painful and difficult. The very structure of our daily life undergoes a profound change, the familiar becomes unfamiliar, and we are lonely.

We need to realize that a loved one who has departed does not want us to be hurt. How can we avoid it? We will mourn for a while; it is a completely natural reaction to what has happened. Then, out of respect for the loved one, we must pick up the pieces of our life and move forward.

The best way to do this is to look ahead, not backward. Knowing our loved one wants the best for us, it behooves us to cooperate with life. This includes our seeking interaction with other people and new directions of life. These things do not lead to forgetfulness. They beckon us to a renewal of life's energy.

I can go on. I will go on.

"When I was fifty, after many years of marriage and three children, my husband finally admitted he was having an affair. Unfortunately, he was unwilling to give her up and the marriage was broken."

~

There's an ancient story about a king by the name Canute who walked down to the seashore one day and ordered the waves to cease.

Like King Canute, we can't exert power over forces of nature or life. There are thing we'd like to change that we can't. There's a big drought and we need rain; beating a drum won't bring it; we wait. Someone falls in love with someone whom we consider to be the wrong person; we can't do anything about it.

When unwanted things happen to us, we need to ask ourself the question: Where do we go from here? If we must adapt ourself to a whole new ball game, let's start adapting. If we're going to have to start over, let's get started. It only adds to pain when we become fixated on a situation that we cannot change. It's best to move as forthrightly as possible in a new set of possibilities.

I'll start from here to the place I must go.

"Look, if a man asked me out it wouldn't necessarily be to dance in my mascara, or even necessarily to stay up all night. Maybe he'd love nothing in the world better than to fall asleep in my arms at nine-thirty."

~

The so-called simple things are what most of us want. Yet we like to deny it, play fire with images of glamour, and give other people the wrong idea of what we want.

Part of the problem lies in our own insecurity. What would someone else think of us if we took off our mask and showed our naked face? Would others laugh at us if they knew we wanted an honest hug instead of a trip to the moon?

Our vulnerability makes us sensitive, so we wear a mask in order to protect ourselves from possible hurt. We keep running in the same futile circle. But if we know what we want, it's self-destructive not to share it with others instead of living a lie. Maybe nobody will laugh at us at all. We can find what we want by sharing our feelings with others.

I'll take a good hug over a trip to the moon anytime.

"I would rather be dead than look like a homey, frizzy white-haired Grandma in a house dress, holding a cake."

~

Why are we so threatened by the way other people appear? Why are we so cruel to them?

I think it's because we fear part of ourself that, for some inexplicable reason, we see in them. Maybe it's a part of self that we don't want to acknowledge or want others to perceive. It embarrasses us. We don't like it or know how to deal with it.

So, our way of denying our feelings is to strike out against someone whom we think resembles that part of ourself we're rejecting. It can get complicated. But what we're doing is grossly unfair and also absolutely futile. We need to bring the disliked part of ourself out into the open, share it—accept it. After that, we no longer need to project our rage at self onto other people. The rage is gone.

I'm going to celebrate the uniqueness of other people, applaud their diversity, and simply enjoy knowing them.

"I feel old, helpless, and rejected. I love my daughter, but she won't talk to me or answer my letters."

∿

All of us like the feeling of being in control. So it's painful when we can't be. It's downright maddening when a wished-for letter or phone call is denied us.

Worse, we may not understand why someone is treating us this way. It's natural to overreact, become angry or even obsessed, try to force a showdown, demand an explanation.

However, this ignores what the other person is feeling or thinking. We don't know. If we assume we know, that's just an assumption. In truth, the other person may be busy or preoccupied; ashamed and unable to deal with guilt feelings; furiously angry; unable to communicate with any clarity; totally unaware of how we feel. After the passing of time, a perfect explanation emerges without any fanfare. What is required of us? Patience.

I'm not going to let life treat me like a leaf on a storm-tossed tree. I won't let my emotions be manipulated by chance.

"New friends are very hard to make as I grow older. I have been rejected many times. Thank God, I do have a few long-standing friends."

≈

It's hard to define friends. They just are. Friendship is mysterious because it is seldom logical on the surface. While our friends can be so utterly different from us, still they're close and supportive.

Most of us have had certain friends for many, many years. It can seem forever. We grew together in lots of ways, shared innumerable experiences, and know one another intimately. We love such friends more than we like them at particular moments. There is a deep level of trust. Support in time of need is guaranteed.

New friends need to be developed, too. However, we grow lazy, wondering if we have the necessary time and energy for such an awesome task. We may be less prone to begin a new friendship than mourn one that has passed away. Yet a true friend, new or old, is integral to life itself.

When was the last time I made a new friend? I'm not too old to do it again.

"I'm the resident Grandpa at work, where I've been for thirty years; because I know I have two choices: I can go in complaining or else greet everyone pleasantly."

~

God knows, all of us have things to complain about from time to time. And we do.

The problem is when other people reach a point where they can't stand our complaining anymore. Sometimes we don't know when to stop. Our griping and whining turn into a bad habit. We move into overkill, lose our sense of humor, and become a deadly bore.

How do we feel when others continually bellyache, find nothing good anywhere, and vent their frustration and anger upon us? It is healthy to express feelings, name demons, cry out for justice, and stand up for rights. However it can be unhealthy when we want it all our way, cease to respect the feelings of others, refuse to look at someone else's point of view, and keep shouting so loudly we can't hear what another person is trying to say. We live in a world with other people. We can get along with them or make everybody's life miserable, including our own.

If I make every effort to be pleasant, will I find others more pleasant as well? I'm going to find out.

"Good-byes, I find, are hard."

~

It isn't easy to say hello or good-bye. Each requires a definite action on our part. Each calls us to involvement with other people.

Good-byes happen at leavetakings. From home to go to school for the first time, from home what may be the last time. We are departing en route to somewhere else. Shortly, the present will be the past. What are we leaving, and in search of what? Perhaps we are exchanging security and comfort for risk and raw new adventure. Who knows? We might not even see again a person to whom we're saying good-bye.

Hello can also be terribly risky stuff. If addressed to a new person in our life, does it mean that our life will undergo change? Will we ever say good-bye to the same person? A greeting that signifies change is a symbolic act. We're saying, in effect, that we welcome change and are willing to go with it.

I won't linger over farewell. I'll focus on new meetings. But I'll seek meaning in both.

"I love children and older people the most."

~

We can't, in the framework of our human life, manage to love everybody. It's impossible.

The more specific we are about whom we wish to love, the more we're able to love in a universal sense. We have to love everyone. If we say we love everyone, but don't reveal love to anyone, we've fallen into an abyss of contradiction.

Whom, then, shall we love? I suppose whom we really and truly do love. To begin, we have inner circles of family and close friends. Reaching out, we may come to categories of people, not just individuals. For example, some prefer women, others men. Maybe Brazilians or Italians, Lebanese or Kenyans, Chinese or Irish. The favorite people of some are children or older people. The important thing is to express our love of people by starting with the love of a person. Let the love grow.

I'll express my love for one person today and make it hold all the love I feel for life itself.

"After my husband and I retired we were both there for our children—financially, listening to their problems, baby-sitting—until we found we were being used. The only times they called us were the times when they wanted something."

∾

All of us share the need to reach out and communicate with others when we want something. This is natural. But many of us do not communicate nearly so winningly when we don't want anything. This is unfortunate. It hurts other people's feelings. It creates highly plausible suspicions concerning our motives.

Many also take family obligation very much for granted in times of felt need, asking for a blank check, or housing without a time limit, or the total sacrifice of someone else's personal freedom. To feel we're being used, or taken for granted can resemble being slapped in the face. It is a jolt. We like, most of us, to pitch in and help others in times of need. We also prefer to be treated as human beings, appreciated, thanked—and called just to say hello or chat.

I'll seek to be appreciated for who I am, as well as for what I can do.

"Grandma always said she loved me, but when she died I was left out of her will. She left everything to other children and grandkids. I'm furious. I could have used some of her money to help me get started in a new venture."

∾

Perhaps the final way we can express our wishes, and exercise whatever power we may have, is by means of our last will and testament.

Since a will sums up what we want to do with our life's possessions, some people restrict the recipients to family members. Others cut out family and remember favorite causes or charities. Surprises are found in a number of wills. Strangers or little-known people who had never seemed important turn out to be very, very important to those who died.

Being left out of a will doesn't mean not being loved. Being included in a will isn't necessarily a sign of love at all. Wills are unpredictable, strange, often emotional, more often just businesslike. When we draw up our own will, we should remember it gives us an opportunity for loving—and expressing exactly what we mean by that.

I'll aim to express myself forthrightly and avoid evasion, doubt, and meanness of spirit.

"The mailbox has become my bright spot in the day. I get lots of letters because I write lots of them."

～

A surprisingly large number of older people write lots of letters. This is especially true of homebound people.

It is nice when the mailbox ceases to sit there as an impersonal receptacle and becomes an integral member of the family. It has room for cards, notes, and letters of every size, in every color. Letters are a great way to reach out, touch other lives, disseminate information, and start friendships.

When we're alone or ill, letters take on an entirely different significance. They are lifelines, bringing joy, greetings, and expressions of caring. They seem to be providential gifts. We should never take our letters, or those of others for granted or treat them casually.

What treasured friend have I ignored for too long? I'm going to pick up my pen, and write with my heart, *now*.

"I just pray that I live at least until my mom is gone so I can see she is taken care of."

～

Numerous seers have wisely pointed out that we don't need to go in search of death. It will find us in its own way, its own time.

So, we can't control how long we shall live or when we shall die, unless we take our own life. This means we're unable to make precise plans related to our demise. Many want to live until a child graduates from school or starts a home, a loved one has found security or a parent who is dependent upon our care has departed.

We have no control here. The best we can do is make plans that are as sensible and foolproof as possible. It is a good idea to nurture a sense of well-being instead of anxiety, serenity instead of fear. The projection of negative feelings accomplishes no good purpose and serves to agitate emotions. We can only do our best, give up the illusion of control, and get on with life.

Today, I'll stop trying to control life—and let it be.

"I am enjoying sex at seventy. The secret we have: I bought two sexy nighties. I have the pink one. He wears the blue one. If we sneak away and elope, I won't be a bit surprised."

~

Secrets are wonderful. Often they're about things that are nobody else's business. Yet everybody wants to know secrets.

One of the last of our self-governed preserves is our private life. Here, all of us are monarchs, children of gods and goddesses, kings and queens. We're at home in our castle. It's essential that we keep sacrosanct this splendid preserve. Threatening it, the world encroaches upon our personal rights to an intolerable degree.

Our sexuality, a gift of heaven, is a splendid and natural part of who we are. There can be play, succulent secrets, games of the heart, and a relationship between two people that is a hallmark of each of their lives. Having fun is considered questionable by puritans who want to control what everybody else does in body, mind, and spirit. Fun and play constitute a holy gift to humankind.

There's still room in my life for play.

"Growing older, a lot of people develop such peculiarities that they're hard to deal with and their personalities are intolerable."

~

I like to visit the aquarium and see all the different fishes there. They're dazzling in their diversity. They range all the way from a sea horse to a piranha, and in every imaginable color.

Watching human beings reminds me of visiting the aquarium. We are absolutely incredible. We are thin and fat, tall and short, old and young, in various hues of color, and all our personalities represent an unimaginable spectrum of diversity.

It's funny, but one person's idea of normalcy or acceptability is another person's idea of peculiarity. There is simply no norm recognized by everyone. Just look at us. We speak different languages, have different accents, like to eat different foods, come from different places, have different goals, cultivate different tastes, laugh at different things, worship in different ways, and even wear different clothing. Differences aside, we're all human. We need to get along and appreciate one another.

My peculiarities are part of what defines me. They're knots and bumps of experience. I appreciate them in myself, and in others.

"My seventy-two-year-old mother eats better than I do, practices yoga, and goes to two aerobics classes a week. But she completely resigned herself to never having sex again after she and my father divorced ten years ago. She tried dating, but it's really hard for an educated older woman to meet interesting men who aren't scared off."

~

We can't, despite our best intentions, prescribe what is best for someone else. We mistakenly try to project our own ideas and feelings onto another person whom we love, yet really don't know as well as we think we do.

Anyone's sex life, or seeming lack of it, is a highly individual matter. Some people don't have sex but channel their sexual energy knowingly and creatively into areas of work, friendship, recreation, and volunteerism.

Separating sex and love is difficult for a number of people who don't want one without the other. And there are women and men who loved deeply once, but feel unable or unwilling to enter into love again. We need to respect people's individual differences when it comes to sex and love, and support them in any way we can.

I'll try to give acceptance and support even when I don't fully understand another person.

"I have acquaintances but no friends. I used to hope that one day a friend would appear. Now, a senior citizen for years, I have lost that hope."

∾

Who is a friend? It takes one to know one. The best way to have friends is to be a friend. It's not a terribly complicated affair. We can try reaching out to others instead of waiting for them to reach out to us.

In other words, initiate the act of giving. Does this make us vulnerable? Yes. Is it a risk? Definitely. Yet without vulnerability and risk, life isn't worth living. How good a friend are we? Are we patient, loyal, open to changes, resistant to gossip, nonjudgmental, ever present in times of someone else's need?

Perhaps we drive away potential friends by our own self-preoccupation, seeming indifference, coldness, and apparent lack of interest in their feelings. If a new friend appears in the distance, and comes closer, try to greet this unique person with warmth and caring. The best thing to do? Appear as a new friend to someone else.

Friendship is a sacred gift. I'll honor it.

"Say kind things—not lies, but true kind things."

∾

Our tongue can be a formidable weapon. Gossip that starts on the wind can become a killer of a tornado.

Unkind things get too frequently uttered. It's somewhat akin to the fact that good news is not considered news. For example, a peaceful protest march of three hundred thousand people may rate four paragraphs in a small news story on page thirty of a metropolitan newspaper; yet a stabbing that takes place during the march will probably move the story to page one.

If we want to get someone else's attention, it's sad that a violent, shocking, and yes, unkind story is more apt to succeed than a tender and kind one. A firecracker is more effective than a hand on a shoulder in arousing an immediate response.

I'll wait before I speak, weigh the circumstances, and let a more peaceful world begin with me.

"I find it's so hard trying to communicate with other people. When I think I'm succeeding, I find I'm not. Strangely, often I am when I am unaware of it. Is there some secret here that is eluding me?"

~

I'm tired of people who take passing note of me then construct a convenient image of their own choice and claim to know me. Aren't you tired of this in your own life, too?

Some people like to idealize us; others denigrate us. Seldom do they draw close enough to see the wounds we bear, the joys we have to share. It can be frustrating, even maddening on occasion.

We are ourselves guilty of the same thing. We pass by too quickly, making a judgment without stopping to learn the truth. We create an image that denies another person's real humanity. We move on and avoid an honest relationship. At times we place someone on a pedestal we have built; at other times we subject a person to painful criticism and gossip, without pausing to know the flesh-and-blood reality. Let's change, and make effort to know one another.

I'll look closer at one I thought I knew. I'll peer more diligently at a new face. I'll make the effort to *know* another.

"I had to cope with being a widow and found helping others is my answer. If I have something to look forward to, and someone who needs me, I feel better."

~

When we're hurting and in need, our immediate salvation is to get outside ourselves. Grieving is natural and necessary, yet it is important to place it in perspective.

It is possible to become obsessed by grief. To look inward and to the past. To feel our energy sapped. To have no reason to get up in the morning. To want to retreat into an opium den-like ambience, move into forgetfulness, embrace fantasy.

Life awaits. Others need us. There is work to be done that only we can do. Our love is needed. Our sense of hope is required where otherwise there might be no hope. Our contribution is essential. We matter. We can make all the difference. We feel better when we have the courage to respond to a need, and look forward to it.

"Caring for my elderly father often makes me very upset. Then he gets upset. Then my husband tells me I'm cruel to my father."

～

Intergenerational relations can be subtle and complex. Often roles are reversed when, for example, a parent moves into the dependent position of a child, and a child suddenly realizes he or she has assumed parental responsibilities.

Caring for anyone is a tricky business. It involves our attitude as well as our work. In caring, do we feel that the person we are helping is vastly inferior to us, or manipulating us, or taking advantage of us? Does caring irritate us or stir up resentments? Is it, in our view, a waste of our time, an intrusion on our life, an exercise in futility? Does the person we are caring for seem ungrateful?

Feelings need to be sorted out. Do we really want to care for someone else? What are the ground rules? Is it possible to have amicable terms of mutual communication?

I'll credit myself for the care I give others. And I'll replenish that ability to care by caring for myself.

"I am an eighty-year-old widower living with my 'family' of five cats and a large dog."

~

Some people make a big mistake when they limit friends to the human race. Other friends, including animals, birds, and fish are available. Dogs and cats seem to be our most frequent companions.

While a dog wags its tail in devotion, a cat rotates a tail in restlessness. A dog licks our hand as a sign of affection, while a cat sits on our lap and scratches our knee. Both have healthy appetites. We must bathe our dog, where as our cat attends personally to such an intimate matter. Each one knows instantly when it has done the right or wrong thing. One is salt, the other pepper.

Our dogs and cats are wonderful friends. A cat is easily put-out and impatient with us, mysterious and puzzling. It wakes us at dawn by getting up on our pillow and purring. A dog is quite patient, hardly ever selfish (except at mealtimes), and easy to live with (although surprisingly hurt). Dogs and cats are good family members.

I'm grateful for the family I have.

"I often use the word phony to describe someone whom I dislike or oppose. Maybe I need to bring phony closer to home."

◇

Some people set us off as if we were a firecracker. We dislike them instantly. Nothing they say or do is likely to meet with our acceptance. Of course, we're capable of setting off the same reaction in other people, too.

Phony is one of the most convenient epithets around. Like a large blanket, it covers a lot of territory. When we completely disagree with a politician, detest the work of a particular artist, or are out to get a neighbor, phony is perhaps the most effective charge to hurl. It's a bit like crying "Fire" in a crowded theater. It evokes attention, sounds an alarm.

However, how do we feel when someone accuses us of being phony? It's a tough charge to answer with clarity because, by virtue of its ambiguity, it is virtually unanswerable. It's buckshot. It's meant to clobber a person, to strike violently, batter and defeat. Let's banish *phony* from our vocabulary, try to understand, and say what we mean.

I'll take others as they are.

"Two of the most important words in the world are thank you."

∼

Insecurity, shyness, and pride often stand in our way when we want to say *thank you*. When we learn how, though, we can build bridges between people.

Expressing thanks is not at all a Pollyanna-ish or sentimental thing to do. It requires grit, earnestness, and hard work, and can be complicated. For example, it isn't always easy for us to accept thanks. This is because we are acutely aware of our shortcomings and often feel unworthy of being thanked.

We need to say *thank you* to others more often that we do. To a stranger who helps us and whom we will probably never see again. To a co-worker who manages a smile of greeting every day for ten years, listens to our problems, and offers support. To a friend who is present in a moment of our great need, and comforts us. To a teacher who patiently works with us, finding promise hidden deep within us, and makes us see it, too. To someone close to us who loves us, and whom we have simply taken for granted.

I have much to be grateful for. Where there's someone to thank, I'll voice my gratitude. I won't leave something so important unsaid.

"In an exceptionally bright moment of truth I realized I was being treated as a thing instead of a person. How can I survive when impersonality leaps out at me?"

∾

We have to. Impersonality leaps out at most of us several times a day.

It is essential to know we are a person. This, when without warning somebody starts to treat us as a thing. What is a thing? An impersonal object. A body in somebody else's way. Someone whose feelings are denied. We are being treated as a thing when nobody cares. When we cry, and nobody listens. When we laugh, and nobody shares it. When people want to make money off us, but don't give a damn about us. When, instead of being appreciated as us, we are regarded simply as a burden, an obstacle, a problem, a number, a cipher.

The best way to deal with the problem is to turn it around. To listen when someone cries. To share someone's laughter. To appreciate another, endeavoring to see a person, neither a problem nor a burden. To be aware of human feelings, and respond to them directly.

I'll greet impersonality with character. I'll respond as a human being and expect to be treated the same.

"I told myself over many years that my life was empty without someone else in it. But I'm in it! My life is not empty at all. I'm grateful for its fullness."

~

Make your move! It's time. Dead ends are not very pleasurable or productive places to be. They are not springboards of hope, are they? It's good to trade them in for something better.

It's easy for us to construct a fantasy about needing a "someone" to make us happy. It is a cop-out. It relieves us of the responsibility to get to work creating our own happiness. All we need (we say) is for Mr. Right or Ms. Right to appear, the ideal figment of our imagination. According to the script, he or she will just walk into our life spontaneously, solve our problems, give us a rush of ecstasy and a glimpse of eternal joy, and we'll live happily ever after.

Oh. It isn't like that, is it? Sure, someone can hand us a gift of pleasure (usually laced with a bit of sadness, too) but no one else can make us happy. It's not up to anyone else. It's up to us.

Today, I'll think about what happiness means for me.

"Most of us can do little about the situation in the Middle East or Central America, but there are many shut-ins who are alone and would love a friendly visit, a trip to the grocery store, or even a phone call."

~

There is so much we can do. It is selfish and self-defeating to sit on the sidelines and refuse to participate in life.

Some of us will want to concentrate on precisely what we can do about the situation in the Middle East or Central America or another part of the world whose problems matter a lot to us. We can organize around a particular issue, bring pressure to bear on politicians, raise funds, request the media to provide information, and help bring about needed change.

Others will wish to volunteer our time and effort closer to home. Here, human needs surround us. There is someone waiting to receive a friendly visit from a good listener. Someone who needs food. Someone who needs a ride. There is someone waiting who desperately needs contact with a human being who cares, wants to help, and is willing to be a friend.

I refuse to sit on the sidelines.

"I wonder why we elderly folk are so stubborn and self-centered. Why can't we love our kids enough to give up our own desires and make it easier for all?"

≈

It is human nature to be stubborn and self-centered. It is love that opens us up to compromise, flexibility, and feeling a concern for others. Elderly people are no more or less stubborn and self-centered than anyone else.

When we feel ignored, neglected, and hurt, it's natural for us to become self-centered. Survival dictates that if no one else cares for us, we must make up for their lack of caring. If we don't, who will?

All of us have a right to our desires. Older women and men should not give up desires any more than anyone else. Compromise is desirable. It happens when any of us is able to fulfill our desires without standing in the way of others to do the same. But no one should ever be asked to bear a disproportionate burden to make it easier for someone else. Sometimes a lack of self-esteem makes us ready to give up our rights. Self-esteem is essential. Keep it up.

I'll compromise where it's desirable, but I'll hold to my desires.

"I will be sixty-nine years old. I have a boyfriend. He is going to be seventy-one. Our sex life is wonderful. For the first time in my life, and after years of a poor marriage, I've had ogasms and climaxes. We both feel like teenagers."

❧

Teenagers might wish to feel so good. Isn't it great that you have found each other, with such happiness as well?

Society has foolishly held a reproving view of seniors as sexless. Or, at least that seniors should be sexless. This grows from a view of sex as intrinsically evil outside of conventional marriage. Rubbish!

Many seniors are widows or widowers. A number are divorced. Often their families like to assume they are disinterested in sex, without libidinous desire. Love and sex are God-given gifts to human beings. Seniors wish to partake of them and participate fully in life. The puritanical, narrow, judgmental view that seniors should be sexless is an outrage against the human spirit. Stereotyping seniors, it seeks to deprive old women and men of life, liberty, and the pursuit of happiness.

What's age-appropriate? Today, I'll let go and play.

"To live alone is better than making a bad choice and suffering the consequences. I have seen friends suffer untold misery with someone unsuitable, unsupportive, and unstable."

~

We're all so different. Universal prescriptions for happiness cannot be handed out over the counter. For some people, to live alone is the best thing to do; they find fulfillment in life without a close partner. For others, to live alone is fatal; a relationship is a necessity.

We need to figure out exactly what kind of person we are. If we're better off alone, let's try to have the courage and insight to make a creative life based on that truth and avoid the torture chamber of a doomed relationship. However, if we're better off living in a relationship with someone else, let's try to find someone who fills the bill. Above all, let's grow up—at whatever age.

Today, I'll think about who I am and what it is I want. I'll prepare to be surprised.

"Loneliness is terrifying. I leave a light burning all night in a small room adjoining my bedroom, but still I awaken scared to death and my loneliness is overwhelming."

∼

Keep the light burning. Loneliness is understandable. We need to handle it the best way we can.

We can also ask the question: Why am I suffering such an overwhelming sense of loneliness? Do I miss terribly a spouse or loved one who has died? Is aging, for example, deeply threatening to me? Am I confronting the idea of my own mortality? What scares me?

Learning how to be by oneself—yet not feel acutely alone—is a great gift. Some find companionship in books, others in music or a garden; still more cherish pets, friends who are nearby, pen pals, activities that carry them outside their immediate environment for a certain amount of time. All of us need to seek and find the companionship we need.

I'll make myself open to all the companionship and community surrounding me in this life.

"People think it's morbid to read the obituaries. Wait'll they lose a mate. I read them every day, looking for men who died at the same age as Rob. I have to read them. Now that I know about grief, I can't seem to ignore it."

~

The best newspapers print wonderful obituaries, filled with highlights of a person's life, colorful details, occasional anecdotes, and a true sense of personality and character. It is a final homage, a public appreciation, a celebration of the incredible uniqueness of a particular human being.

Someday people may read our obituary. It's not morbid at all to read obituaries. Quite the contrary. They're indispensable accounts concerning the passage of life. They're stories that help to provide a chronicle of time.

It's time we were all more honest about obituaries. Reading them represents the opposite of denial of grief. When we know about grief and have survived it, an obituary is a life connection for us. Encountering someone else's past, we may acknowledge our own passing that is in progress. We can honestly mourn someone whom we have loved, and make our mourning positive by celebrating the life with joy and gratitude.

Today, I'll think about the passing of lives. I'll look for the connections—and celebrate, honor, and renew my commitments.

"My husband died eight months ago. I can't accept the fact that he's not coming back. I can't live without him. He was everything to me. I cry all the time. I cry when I go to bed and reach out and there is only a pillow there."

∼

Grief is a natural reaction to loss. It is healthy to grieve, to grant expression to feelings, and let go of a rigid, stoical control.

However, there comes a time when grief should run its course. Life beckons to us once again. Other people need our time and attention. The loved one who has died undoubtedly wants us to experience the richness and fullness of life, not stay imprisoned in sadness.

It is not an act of disloyalty to a departed loved one to start life anew. It is an act of deep loyalty precisely because it is an act of living. A loved one who has departed does not want us to embrace death prematurely, or turn our back on living, or exist inside a mausoleum. Let life come.

I'll cry when I must, and then I'll stop, open my eyes, and start looking for new possibilities.

"I'm single and older, have a good job, and have taken on many interests. But hey, life without that special person is very, very difficult."

∼

Yearning for companionship is one of the most natural things in the world. But many people are single. Some always were, others are widows and widowers, still others are divorced. Ironically, a lot of people in relationships yearn to be singles.

Is the grass always greener on the other side? The answer seems to be that, regardless of whether we are with someone else or alone, we need to find ways that lead to self-fulfillment. A book entitled *The Lonely Crowd* explored how being with other people does not always seem to provide a solution. For the vast majority of us, no one person can ever bring total fulfillment into our lives.

Taking this a step further, the poet Marianne Moore pointed out that the cure for loneliness is solitude. We have to deal with ourselves. We must learn how to be alone, handle the demons, and find peace. Staying busy or becoming dependent upon someone else will not provide it.

I'm going to get used to being with myself, even when I'm also with others.

"*One of my two grown daughters is a lesbian, and lives with another woman; the other's in prison. I simply told them they'd both made some bad choices. Now only my daughter in prison will write to me.*"

∾

One of the saddest things in the world is isolating ourselves from those who won't let us run their lives for them.

When we demand the right to control others' lives on our own terms, we are practicing conditional love. But there isn't any such thing. It's a contradiction. True love is unconditional. It contains no conditional clauses.

If we try to love, but also wish to dictate the terms of another person's life, we've embarked on an impossible situation. It's a bit like trying to be an absolute monarch, an old-fashioned king or queen, in a democratic society. To love means to trust. Anyone who's truly loved knows he or she is trusted with life. There is a deep awareness that love will never be withheld under any circumstances.

If I love, why must I judge? Today, I'll embrace those I care about. I'll try accepting without condition.

48

"Be a good friend. When you have a good day get on the phone and make plans. Don't cancel them. Value your plans. Remember, to have good friends you must be a good friend."

≈

Friends are the staples of life. We should make vows to friends, cherish them, offer thanks for them.

But we often treat friends cavalierly, taking them for granted. We take, take, take while failing to give. We expect friends to be there for us in moments of need, while we may fail to be present for them at similar times. Sometimes we exaggerate our friends' faults and blemishes, while we adamantly refuse to extol their virtues or offer them praises.

I suppose the reason is that we're so close to real friends that we treat them as we might old shoes. They're here, reliable, tested, comfortable, and faithful. So we're not necessarily on our best behavior with them as we would be with party guests. We're sure they'll understand, without explanation.

We're better friends when we treat our friends better.

Today, I'll think about the people I love, and why. I'll pick up the phone or write a letter, now, and tell them so.

"Why can't a child return to a parent even a bit of the love that has been poured out unselfishly and at great sacrifice?"

~

Love is hard to measure. At times our human roles get in the way. In the place of a human being we perceive only a certain role: mother, father, daughter, son, wife, husband, or grandparent.

It's necessary to see a flesh-and-blood person beneath each role. One reason we don't is that roles themselves create all sorts of expectations. Why did my mother act that way and embarrass me? Why did my father cut the ground out from under me when I needed his understanding and support? How could my daughter have betrayed me by doing that? How can I ever forgive my son after what he did to me? My granddaughter had no right to criticize me. When I needed my granddad to be warm and loving, he was judgmental and cold.

All the above reactions stem from role expectations. All of us need to free ourselves, and other people deeply connected to our lives, from mere role playing. It is essential to be as honest as possible about our real identities, our feelings and motives, our real expectations, our real possibilities.

Today, I'll give everyone a clean slate. I'll look beyond what's owed or expected. I'll start with my love, and go from there.

"For forty-five years I blamed my lack of friends on the fact that I am overweight. Then I decided to be friendly toward people rather than wait for them. It worked. I found most people don't care about looks."

∼

It can take a lifetime to make such a simple discovery. A big reason is that we live in a society where image is often considered more important than reality.

This, combined with the emergence of a youth cult in the media, leads to an emphasis on an unrealistic ideal of physical attractiveness. So being merely pretty takes precedence over being truly beautiful. Form is given credence over content. Many try to emulate or even become an image. This leads to tragedy when the self gets lost, despised, or rejected and a person becomes alienated from who he or she is.

The result is that we see a lot of robots running around, along with armies of stereotypes and legions of shadows on our streets. It's such a marvelous release to recognize that we are stunningly human, incredibly individual, fashioned in love, and free to be ourselves.

I'll look in the mirror and smile. I'll greet myself as I would someone I love.

"When you're older, people expect you to be either a prude or a dirty old man. In fact, I'm as interested in sex as I ever was—and as disinterested."

≈

When sex is identified solely with the rites of youth, it is ludicrously misunderstood.

Sex is as natural as breathing. It is a universal gift and an integral part of creation. But older women and men are frequently seen in an unnatural way and denied their humanity.

The stereotyping that takes place is both ridiculous and utterly wrong. "Older people are no longer sexual," it's affirmed. Or, "It's disgusting to see an older person who still spends time and energy on sex. Their minds should be on higher things unless they're dirty and perverted." Or the opposite: "Older people are judgmental, puritanical, rigid, and opposed to sex. They've forgotten what it means to be human." Our society stands in need of considerably more sex education and enlightenment. We need a lot more honesty and awareness.

I've a right to my loving thoughts. With love and encouragement, I'll express them.

"I've always had friends much younger than myself. I'm in my seventies now, and I have a group of friends in their twenties and thirties who seem to live my stories, who take me out and spoil me. Sometimes, though, I wonder if they just want to inherit my house."

~

Friendships across lines of ethnicity, race, sex, and age are the most natural things in the world. They should be enjoyed and celebrated. They reaffirm what is best about the human spirit.

However, many of our lives have been touched by prejudice of one sort or another, including negative attitudes toward people who are different from us. Often we've been taught to fear them. Or not to trust them. This is terribly unfortunate.

It's good to remember that the only thing we need fear is fear itself. This allows us to know other people as potential friends, not enemies; to be trusting; and to let go of debilitating thoughts that are harbingers of fear.

I'll take people as they are. I'll err on the side of trust. I can't waste the gift of a single friendship.

∼ Memories ∼

"I worship my dad. However, he's an absolute stranger to me. I'm in my thirties, ambitious, work too hard, but am determined to get to the top. My dad had a chance for success when he was young, blew it, and ended up a guy who's hurting and bruised. He's a has-been. I want to make it big for the both of us."

∼

We can't go all the way back in our history, or anyone else's, and rewrite it.

Nor can we assume we understand anyone else's past or how best to deal with it. A principal reason is that many herstories and histories include emotional traumas, painful breakups and divorces, difficult professional experiences, and unresolved dilemmas that we can't see.

It's particularly dangerous if we think we understand someone else's pain when we actually don't. The next fatal step is to prescribe a solution for the person on the basis of our flawed analysis. We may offer encouragement, support, friendship, solace, time, energy, and love—but the buck has to stop here when we feel like playing god.

Today, I'll take a hard look at what drives me. I'll accept the limits of what I can do.

"*All of us always thought my father was a neat guy. He died last year. Now mom has told us he was bisexual and slept with a number of men as well as women. She said he also misused alcohol and sometimes beat her. She is fit to be tied because she repressed her feelings for so long.*"

~

One of the biggest mysteries of them all—right up there with Sherlock Holmes and *Murder, She Wrote*—is why people repress feelings over a long period of time.

It requires so much energy to repress feelings! And, worst of all, the feelings that got repressed have to surface somewhere else, with Lord knows what ramifications and repercussions.

Think of the damage done, the sadness caused because reality was not confronted openly and mutually, with the hope that something practical could be done about the whole thing. Why don't we learn, and not repeat old tragedies?

I won't shroud any part of my life in darkness. I'll leave behind no hurtful surprises.

"Lately I've found myself thinking of a man I loved nearly thirty years ago. Somehow, despite all the intervening events, I realize I never loved anyone else so purely and totally as I loved him. I'd give anything to be able to find him again and tell him so."

～

An ideal, especially one in the past, can seem purer than the driven snow, untainted by the pressures and necessities of life.

It's all right for us to hold onto such an ideal, and give it a place in our life, as long we connect it to reality. For example, we may remember fondly, even passionately, someone we loved many years ago. In our present recollection, he ore she may seem nearly perfect.

But no one is. Over the passing years we've changed, radically and in endless small ways. So has the person we remember, who may no longer be alive; or, if living may be in a happy, stable relationship. More to the point, it is not fair to compare our past idea with a flesh-and-blood person presently in our life. It's far more important to love the person who is *here*.

I won't judge the present by the past. The past may seem perfect; the present is here. Today, I welcome it with open arms.

"Do you think we'll ever get back to the land of our dreams?"

∼

Nostalgia beckons in all of our lives. It's as if there were an archetypal dream we all share, filled with old-fashioned virtue and rugged adventure, and it tugs hard at the edges of our reality.

Yet the dream needs to be alive in the present, filled with the most compelling contemporary images as well as fragments from our past imagination. Our necessity is to live fully in the present. An understanding of the past is absolutely necessary, but romanticizing it can prove deadly.

We cannot get back to anything. As the author Thomas Wolfe pointed out, we can't go home again. Sometimes we want it so badly that we can see an old house as if it were here in the present, smell past kitchen warmth, look at smoke rise from a chimney. It's essential for us to honor the past, and love what is best about it, while using that experience to forge ahead in our present life.

What would it take to make this the land of my dreams? How could I come closer? Today, I'm thinking of how to get there, not how to go back.

"I could never forgive my father for walking away from our family when I was a kid. He deserted us, my mom, sister, and brother. I grew up, went to school, then went to work and got married. I always hated him for what he had done. Recently I went to visit him. He was very sick and about to die. We bonded at last. It gave me peace."

~

Life is full of fierce passions, big hurts, great joys, and lots of things beyond any easy understanding.

It's inevitable that we respond to life as passionately as life treats us. We say we'll "never forgive." We say we'll "fight to the finish." We say we're "bruised, bloodied, but unbowed." We say we'll "kill for what's right."

Our fiercest passions, however, seem gradually to give way to a glimmer of empathy and a streak of tenderness. We remember the good, not only the bad. We even learn to laugh in recollection of a difficult past event, instead of crying about it. Our focus shifts. It is an indication of maturity. It permits us to partake of the riches.

Today, I'm going to scrutinize an old wound and find forgiveness.

"I'm an eighty-seven-year-old man. My wife and all five of my brothers and sisters have died, as have two of my three children. What's the point in living when nearly everyone I love is gone?"

～

Life isn't over until it's over. But there are times—we may be twenty or seventy, forty or eighty—when we ask: What is the point in living?

Moments when we ask this question tend to be crucial turning points. We may have had our professional life wiped out or lost a job. We may have ended a marriage or loving relationship, or lost a child or partner in death. Maybe we feel we've run out of steam, have nowhere to go, and can't make it.

So we ask: How can I get from here to there? From today to tomorrow? The middle of the night to the next morning? Sunrise to sunset? At our worst moment everyone we love seems to be gone, along with out own self-esteem, our very faith and hope. But before long something curious happens. Hope beckons. Life stirs again. We realize the point in living is living itself.

Today I start small. I'll make life itself reason to live.

"My husband and I played Scrabble every Sunday with a much younger couple for many years. We watched their kids grow up. One day they just stopped returning our calls, as if we'd never existed. I guess we were too old."

~

An old adage goes something like this: "Everybody is odd but me and thee. And some days I think thou art odd, too."

Human nature is far more unpredictable than the strangest weather pattern can ever be. All of us surprise others at times by our actions. We cause joy and jubilation, hurt and dismay.

We need to realize other people's actions that jolt us are usually not capable of easy analysis. Such actions tend to defy logical, rational explanation. They are buried deep in psychological matter. Since we don't understand, we should avoid making assumptions. A good friend of mine has two words framed and displayed prominently on his desk: ASSUME NOTHING. This comes close to being the best advice in the world.

Today, I stop looking for a reason for the hurts I've sustained. And start healing.

"I have just begun to realize what a terribly dysfunctional family I grew up in. I'm fifty, my mother is going on seventy, and I am so filled with rage at her that I can't stand to see her or talk to her. I detest her and what she did to hurt me as a child."

~

We make a big mistake when we attempt to look at life in terms of starkly contrasting shades of black and white, period, instead of discerning all kinds of mixed images in subtle and overlapping grays.

Life is made up of gradations instead of absolutes. All of us make mistakes, big ones. We have good intentions that go awry sometimes, and work our very well at other times.

It is self-defeating to designate someone as the enemy, and absolve ourself from any involvement in a bad situation. Unless we can work through our anger and rage toward another person, it is we who suffer more than anyone else. Often a quality that we detest in another person is one imbedded deep in ourself.

Today, I'll look calmly to the source of my anger. Would I live differently free of it?

"At sixty-nine I can look back and understand that all my problems were fear-based, nameless fears that caused me untold agony and mental anguish."

≈

We need to deal with fears when they arise in our life, one by one—confront them and try to transform them. When we don't they have a tendency to gang up on us. It's a dismaying sight to look out and see a gang of fears bearing down on us. Fears multiply quickly, feeding on one another. A climate of fear makes it easy for them.

So, it's smart to learn how to take on one fear at a time. Analyze it. Figure out how it gets to us, crippling us and reducing us to shivers. We need to break the hold a fear has on us. Most fears are irrational. Anything that can terrify us and break our will is an enemy. Our mature lives have no room for this kind of decidedly unfriendly force.

What frightens me? Today, I face my fears head-on, and move beyond them.

"I am seventy-one and have lost all trust in my husband, who has betrayed me with another woman. We are still together because it is financially impossible to separate. I feel hurt, depressed, humiliated, unwanted, unloved, and without hope."

∾

We are never meant to live at the whim of someone else, no matter how close. Our own life is of inestimable importance.

To feel betrayed is awful. But sometimes there are circumstances we don't fully understand. We may even have contributed unwittingly to the problem in some way. If the matter can be discussed openly, every aspect of the situation brought out, this can prove valuable.

When all else fails, other people may need to enter in, attempting to mediate, seek alternatives, work out ways in which a seemingly impossible situation may somehow become a possible one.

Forgiveness is about forgiving, not about the magnitude of the crime. Today I'll reclaim what's mine with forgiveness and love.

"My greatest fear is of losing my memory. I'm living for today, but I'm also sort of walking testament to my dead lover. If I forget his story—the way he smiled— he's just gone, lost."

～

Other lives are contained in our own. Their stories are interwoven with ours. Their memory rests in ours.

This keeps us going when we might otherwise give up quietly. A lot rides on our shoulders. We need to pass on to new generations the stories we've shared, names and faces, challenges and battles, victories and losses, and the love we knew.

We are most alive when we're engaged in being a walking testament. It takes our mind off our own worries and bruises, letting us share a wider and brighter vision of life. We live not just for ourself, but for others, too. This adds dimension and meaning to our life, making it richer and more purposeful.

Whose are the stories that I carry? Today, I'll take stock of that trust. I'll draw on the strength it offers.

"I know seniors who can't stop suffering over the loss of a child decades ago, or their parents' divorce back in history. They spend mental and emotional time wishing things could be 'put back the way they used to be,' no matter how fruitless this is."

～

Some people can't seem to get over the past. A divorce or a death still haunts them, bringing up great unhappiness and causing distress.

We need to let ghosts have their long-desired peace. They wander restlessly through our life, from attic to cellar, and only we can free them. They disrupt out life, but we hold firmly onto them as if they were an obsession.

To free them means to let them leave at last. They have been imprisoned in our memory too long. Some of them may go back all the way to our childhood. They represent things that we never allowed ourself to resolve or make peace with. The time has come. When they are free, so are we.

Today, I'll make a conscious effort to deal with past unhappiness. Enough! I'll let it go.

"My husband and I lived together for forty years. He died three years ago. Most nights I wake up to see him coming down the hall. Sometimes he looks sad, sometimes angry."

~

Our life can become almost totally intertwined with the life of someone we love.

Year after year we did the same things together, thought similar thoughts, shared food and drink, sex and love, opinions and ideas, hugs and nurturing, joys and friends, disappointments and defeats, travel and our home.

When parting comes, it is devastating. It seems that no one else can really understand the depth of it. A basic part of our self is gone. But then, another part remains. We see our beloved, speak and hear, feel the presence close to us. We look forward to being reunited in a fuller sense. We are more grateful than angry, content than sad.

I won't forget the ones I've lost. But I'll go on.

"I married my high school sweetheart and soon we will celebrate our golden anniversary. But I always thought my sister was the pretty one and I was ugly. Last week my husband said, 'I always thought you were the prettiest girl in the class and I still do.' Why, oh why, could he not have said that fifty years ago?"

~

If only we could say at all the times exactly what we think. There would be far less confusion. Of course, this has a darker side, too. There might be small wars all over the place. Yet clarity is to be sought in every situation. "Why did he say that?" "Why didn't he tell me that?" "There's something drastically wrong and I can't get to the bottom of it." "If we could all just put our cards on the table, we could work this out fast."

In the tangled jungle of verbiage, many times we fail to pay a compliment that we intend to offer. We swallow a badly needed explanation, one that can clarify a difficult situation. It's too bad when we can't say what we think.

I want to minimize hurt and confusion in my life. I'll speak up. I won't hold back.

"People who are aging now came from an era that believed in keeping problems to themselves. They didn't let others know when they were depressed or hurting over money and health problems."

∼

I can remember when my grandmother confronted a terminal illness. I was a teenager. She confided in me, gave me a letter to be shared with others after her death, and told no one else.

Grandma believed in conveying an example of strength. This meant that she seldom confided in others about her problems. Our life today seems very different. In our age of mass media everybody's story is told to everybody. Secrets are widely publicized and considered juicy.

Yet, despite this flood of information about people, our society is indifferent and uncaring when it comes to meeting the needs of many, including a sizable number of older women and men. Unlike my Grandma, these people tend to let others know when they're hurting and in need. But our society fails them when it refuses to listen, remains aloof, and doesn't care.

When I hurt, I'll say so.

"It's been my experience (I'm to be sixty-four next month) that the old curmudgeon and irascible pessimist and complainer of either sex is a full-blown version of what that person was at twenty or twenty-five."

∽

When we attend a high school or college class reunion, and meet once again people whom we haven't seen for thirty, forty, or fifty years, often we experience a shock of recognition: Some seem exactly the same.

This initial view obscures the reality of deep and fundamental changes in everybody. No one stays the same. In addition to changes in faces and bodies, there are unseen ones in personality, character, and outlook.

Life, of course, can dim humor and blur optimism; it can also bring happiness beyond our expectations, and a great sense of trust. But it isn't life that is the initiator. Instead, it is our response to what occurs in our life. We are never locked into any pattern on the basis of who we once were. What's vital is who we are now.

I won't be chained to my past selves. I'm who the years and my actions have made me.

"I survived a divorce, a single-parent family with two sons who rebelled at the broken home, a former in-law who has been the blight of my existence, an unplanned retirement, and illness. Life goes on, and we can only give it our best shot."

∼

Life can resemble a soap opera. At times it seems that it might at least be preferable to turn it into a grand opera.

So many things happen to us. They pile up like falling snow. We become confused and feel like a car that's been banged up or an ocean liner about to sink on the open seas. What more could possibly happen? We wait, and bam!—something new threatens our equanimity. How long, how long?

Eventually, the school of hard knocks teaches us how to duck the worst punches, dance around the ring, and store up needed energy for the next round. Sometimes this is called maturity. It is accompanied by a seasoned sense of humor, an overall view that's called perspective, and pluck for the lucky who survive.

How have I survived adversity before? What was it that got me through? I know I can do it again.

"Self-pity sneaked into my life again when I wasn't looking. Help!"

~

Self-pity is a hydra-headed monster. It reaches into every part of our life. When we become too self-absorbed, we forget to share our life with others and remain open to helping them.

We fail again, and blame it on mom, dad, school, God, politics, that time we failed an exam in the sixth grade, and the time Uncle Louie got drunk before our high school graduation. Oh yes, we can find plenty of reasons for our failure. The world was never kind to us! We were doomed from the outset.

There are reasons for self-pity. We've been hurt badly in the past. We didn't receive the recognition we deserved. Someone cut us down instead of building us up. What are we going to do about it now? Learn how to accept thanks and recognition, feel adequate instead of inadequate, and seek encouragement.

I expect goodness and wonder. I don't have time for self-pity.

"I want to let go of past sorrows."

∿

Some of us tend to collect past sorrows as if they were treasured objects of glass hidden away on a shelf.

We take them down from time to time, touch them gently, and have a good cry. This one might be a sorrow related to an old romance, an affair of the heart. That one is connected to a life's dream we had once. If we had brought it to fruition, our life today would be very different.

While it's valuable to understand where we've been in the past, it is futile to relive decisions made a long while ago. We've changed since then. Our lives became what they did. Perhaps we need to quit regarding past sorrows as sorrows at all. They are things that happened to us. We learned from them. Now it's time to put away our glass menagerie, that sad but foolishly treasured collection of past sorrows. It belongs to the past.

I honor the past, sorrow and all—but today I'll look ahead, expecting something better.

"After living for so many years my head feels like a haunted house. I have so many ghosts."

~

It's easy to let ourselves become obsessed with a constantly recurring recollection or thought. Dwelling on it, we allow it to enter into our whole being. Slowly, slowly, it takes on the power of the unforgettable.

If our head feels like a haunted house filled with ghosts, we can do something about it. Open up the windows! Swing wide the doors! Fill the haunted house with air and light. Clean out closets and dark corners. Sweep away cobwebs. Scrub floors, Empty useless old objects out of the attic and cellar. Apply fresh paint.

Letting the sunshine in, we can allow the ghosts to leave. It isn't at all hard to do. What is required is determination, making a decision, and following through. Ghosts don't want to remain anymore because they don't feel at home. Our house is no longer haunted. We're free.

Today I'll set my ghosts free.

"I was born in 1904, the third child of seven. I am the only one left of the family. I have known sorrow and grief, but I think everything that happens is for a purpose."

∼

Both terrible and wonderful things happen to most of us. Some people simply believe that anything that happens has a purpose in life. Others feel that events are as random as Christmas tree lights.

In my view, anything that happens can have a purpose. We make use of it in creative, caring, intelligent ways. It can teach us a lesson, grant us a benefit. When an event appears to be a tragedy or disaster, it can help us develop perseverance or courage or patience.

To look at events in our lives in sequence—try to find a meaningful relationship between them—can be profitable. We learn that what had a first seemed to be adversity became an advantage. What appeared to be a big advantage wasn't what we wanted at all.

Today, I see my life as an inevitable progression— everything, good and bad, bringing me to this still moment of gratitude.

"In every older woman you will find a young girl, in every older man a boy."

~

All of us are people, not just parts of people. Our whole lives are wrapped up in who we are. We're walking stories.

This means childhood and youth are parts of the experience of older men and women. So, when we look at them, we need to see as much of their wholeness as we can. For example, I realize that my ninety-five-year-old mother was once a little girl. It helps me understand that quality in her, its natural exuberance and laughter, a certain shyness and innocence.

When we meet an elderly man, we should look for the inquisitive, untamed boy as well as the experienced, refined man. When we meet an elderly woman, we should seek to find the girl and the young woman who remain alive as parts of the wholeness of her nature. Perhaps then she can respond to us from these reflections of her past, animating her presence before our eyes.

I won't be afraid to show the child in me.

"It seems to me we're already dead if we live only in our memories."

∿

Memories are terribly seductive when they insatiably make love to our longings and caress our imaginations.

All of us have memories. It's natural and healthy to welcome and enjoy them. They become a problem, however when they cause us to lose interest in our life right now. This is when we prefer the past. We move into it. Finally, we live in the past.

We can't, though. Trying to makes us become discombobulated to an alarming degree. We're neither fish nor fowl, here nor there. What a mess! If we add an addiction to this, we can find ourselves in serious trouble. The answer is an uncomplicated one. This is it: We need to get up, walk to the nearest window, open it, lean outside, feel a breeze on our face, give a hearty shout, and decide—right now in this very instant—to rejoin the human race.

Today, I resolve to look straight ahead, honoring my memories, but expecting to make new ones.

"Cremains! There are no ashes—they're ground-up bone fragments, if you want to know the truth. I saw my wife die, and whatever became of her next has got nothing to do with that stuff in the box on my mantel."

～

The passage from life to death remains, in nearly everyone's conciousness, the most important journey we ever take.

The passage of a loved one is as compelling to us as our own. We can agonize over this, spend sleepless nights, have troubled dreams. We ask the question: how can we find peace? This question stands out in stark relief. Whether a loved one's body has been buried deep in the earth, or its ashes scattered on the sea or kept in a container, our relationship to the departed is still very much alive.

Have we forgiven anything that might still stand between us that was unresolved? Have we accepted forgiveness for any anxiety or pain that we believe we may have inflicted upon the departed? Have we been able to let go—and let our beloved go freely? We need to grant our loved one Godspeed on his or her journey that now continues. And, finally, we need to accept his or her blessing upon our continuing life here.

The loved one I've lost would wish me happiness, not grief. Today, I'll try to give them that.

"My memories can drive me crazy. Make me feel sad, disturb me, confuse me. I need a new way of dealing with them."

~

Our memories are vast and deep as the ocean. We store virtually everything in our memories: hate and love, horror and beauty, numbness and forgiveness.

When we have loved, the people involved with us can never perish. They live on in our consciousness, our memory. Even when their bodies have undergone burial, our memory of them can never be buried. It keeps them alive in timeless orbit.

We remember. Vividly. Each detail. The past is present. Our childhood comes alive. Personalities in middle school are as present as people we met last week. A loved one, long gone, smiles, laughs, embraces us. There is a raw immediacy linking the past to our present moment. The gusto is real. In fact, the present moment—the now—lacks true recognition without what went before it. The past validates it. In this sense, no one whom we have loved is dead. Our lovers and friends who are gone live in our memory, our recognition, our love in this present moment.

I'll keep my memories alive—seeding them with new ones.

"Let the past go. Be forgiving. Remember that nobody is perfect."

~

Why is this so hard for us to do most of the time? We tend to hug the past as if it were a lover, even when it has caused us untold pain and distress. Why don't we let go of it and live in the present moment? We can keep our memories without letting them control us.

It seems even harder for us to forgive past hurts, real or imaginary betrayals, transgressions, and broken dreams. Sometimes we hold onto an old grudge as if it were a sacred object. We relive an old argument over and over again in our thoughts, summoning it to a position of honor in our mind, playing it over as we would an old video.

The victim of all this is ourselves. We deny our own peace. We permit anger to burst into a hot flame inside us. We keep blaming someone else. Yet we are no more perfect than that hapless person locked in our past. When we are able to forgive him or her, we make a big contribution to our own peace. Our healing begins.

Today, I'll forgive what I had thought was unforgivable. I'll stop punishing myself.

≈ Health ≈

"I'm seventy-one and recently fell and hurt my back. My doctor doesn't want me to drive a car anymore. But my car was my connection to life outside my home. I hate the idea of losing my independence and having to rely on other people for help."

≈

It's an illusion whenever we believe we are free and not dependant on other people.

Our life is tightly networked with the lives of others. We breathe the same air, drink the same water, eat the same food, walk on the same earth, use the same energy, watch the same TV, read the same press, vote in the same election, cheer in the same stadium, get ready for the same departure with death, and share the same enterprise called life.

And all of us rely on others for every possible kind of help. It seems apparent that frontier days, accompanied by their fierce stance of independence, are long-gone relics from the past. It is a sign of maturity to welcome help from others as well as to offer it willingly.

I may have to rely on others. I won't let that become a frightening prospect.

"My aunt is a lively eighty-eight-year-old woman who is a strong survivor, including being stubborn as hell. I look in on her every day, cook for her occasionally, and talk to her on the phone regularly. I'm her only relative. But I wonder if my aunt should continue to live in her home or move to a retirement home. I am the one who apparently must make that decision."

∽

Taking a life a day at a time, and doing the best we can, is a sterling idea.

Sometimes we can't plan ahead effectively. Nor do we need to. We don't know what the future holds. We continue to live in the present, under the best conditions we can muster.

The biggest decision can be the choice to take life a day at a time. This means pouring our available energy into it. We cease second-guessing and looking over our shoulder to see if something is gaining on us. We quit wondering about *this* alternative or *that* one, shuffling them like cards in a deck, and concentrate on feeling gratitude for what we have in the present moment.

I can't control tomorrow. I offer thanks for this period of grace in which I can move and have my being.

"*I have learned to live with pain, but mostly it's prayer. One must try very hard to concentrate on other things.*"

~

Pain can take over our life. It makes incessant demands. It insinuates itself into every part of our being.

To remove it from the center or our life is a salvific thing to do. But we can't just pick it up as if it were an object, and place it elsewhere.

Our mind and spirit provide the way to remove it. We can learn how to focus the center of our attention somewhere else. It's as if we possess a giant spotlight that we slowly turn from shining here to shining there. Prayer and meditation are excellent ways to change our focus. The point is that our attention turns elsewhere. When it does, we are freed from an obsessive concentration on anything that seeks to tyrannize our life.

Today, I'll look for a good distraction. I won't be ruled by pain.

"My self-esteem is sinking, yet I know I have strength or I could not have survived as many emotional and physical blows as I have taken."

∽

Life's wounds strengthen us sometimes, weaken us at others. Wounds by themselves tend to be debilitating. Yet they serve to awaken our spirit and courage.

It's foolhardy to seek out wounds as if they were trophies. They can exact a great price. Usually it requires considerable strength to survive them, and heal. So we need to protect ourself from being wounded as much as possible.

Yet all of us have deep wounds that we live with. To deny them is tantamount to preventing their healing. We need to acknowledge them, share them with others who are close to us, and do everything possible to contribute to their gradual healing. When we can do this, they may become blessings in disguise.

Today, I'll examine my wounds, not with sorrow, but with the pride of a survivor.

"My mother's thoughts are turned only to what she cannot do. She speaks only of her aches and pains and the bleakness of her life. Whatever I try to do for her is met with a negative response and nothing is ever right."

∾

Sometimes we have to do our very best against odds that seem insurmountable.

At such a time it seems to us there is only darkness, no light. The weight upon us is unbearable. We cry out for an answer, but hear only more questions. Like Job, we realize that we find ourself in a crucial moment of trial.

We can only place one foot ahead of the other, and edge slowly forward. Our duty seems to call for a repetition of sameness. We receive no thanks, only criticism. We wonder if what we are doing is right. Sacrificing our energy and time, we'd like to feel appreciated. The difficult time extends itself. Then, sometimes there comes a turning, a change, a positive response. It is enormously helpful, and we are grateful.

In a sea of negativity, I'll endure. I'll watch for a turning point or a positive response—and that will be everything.

"I am caring for my mother who is ailing, forgetful, and negative. Forgetful is the hardest because I must repeat, repeat, and repeat. I try to remember that one day I may also be in need and try to do the best I can for today."

～

To err is human. To forget is a damn nuisance.

Yet, growing older, most of us tend to be more forgetful than we used to be. This means, in practical terms, that it's often necessary for others to repeat what they said. Nothing is intrinsically wrong with that. To repeat seemingly guarantees more grasp of the content. It underscores and underlines.

It's helpful to imagine we're speaking a foreign language when we repeat. It's a language that consists of repeats. So, in order to learn it, we need to repeat and repeat and repeat. No harm is done, it can be a bit of fun, the message gets across, and nobody's feelings get hurt. There's even a bonus. This is good training for us. Our day will arrive when we'll need to hear words repeated. We might as well get used to it.

I may forget things someday too. While I've got the gift of clear memory, I'll strive to be gracious and helpful to those who forget now.

"*If unable to be independent as an older woman, I, for one, would like to be allowed, after adequate counseling and a waiting period, to be given a lethal injection or pills, go to sleep, and not wake up.*"

~

I remember a hit play in the 1960s called *Stop the World, I Want to Get Off*. It expressed humorously the way most of us feel occasionally when life becomes too hectic.

However, we can't stop the world unless we're Superman. And, when it comes to jumping off and leaving the action behind, it's not as simple or easy as it might seem. I don't believe our life belongs exclusively to us in a selfish way. We're in life with other people. It's a community enterprise. We owe life, and other people, something.

The biggest challenge on earth is reinventing the next day. Honoring it. Loving it. Polishing it and making it shine. Other people need us just as much as we need them. We need to embrace life together.

Who are the people I owe, whose lives would be changed without me? I'll think of them today, and of the value to them.

"It isn't easy to discipline a weakened body or a depressed mind, but it can be done. Set your goal to look outside yourself."

～

There are times when looking deeply into self, we encounter the equivalent of a toxic waste dump. We've polluted our own environment, that of our own self.

What can we do? Some give up. Others continue a deplorable process of ravaging self-destruction. Others yearn for recovery.

Recovery is available. It involves looking outside ourself. This lets us see a whole picture in which we're a small part. It helps us find others like ourself. We can share stories, give strength and receive it. We come to realize that hope is something tangible that exists. We discover hidden strengths inside us that we never tapped. We recover self-respect. We find we're not alone at all, but that a circle of acceptance awaits us.

Today, I'll set my sights on something or someone else. I won't brood on myself.

"*My husband at the age of fifty-seven was diagnosed as having Alzheimer's disease. I am sixty-one years old and still enjoy living. My heart is breaking for him and I'm having a difficult time finding my own way in life with a husband in his condition.*"

∿

There comes a time in the case of a terminal or incurable disease when we must do everything we possibly can as a caregiver, and at the same time go on living our life.

To be imprisoned as a caregiver in a way that kills our spirit and stifles our expectation for life is not what we are meant for. The concept of life itself must always include love of self. Whenever we try to repress this, bottle it up and put a tight cap on it, we find it emerges in other parts of our life with sometimes devastating results.

Love of self is not intrinsically selfish. If it's lacking one cannot really love another person in a healthy way. We'll want to do everything possible for a loved one in a terminal or incurable illness. This does not include the human sacrifice of our own life.

I'll give thought to caring for myself today. I can't sustain others without doing so.

"I have AIDS and am in my fifties. My main fear is that I will become a recluse. Work—even aggravating and dismal work—keeps me going."

~

There is a private place hidden away in many of our lives that is potentially reclusive. We find it attractive when we grow weary of repetitiveness, especially when the repetition seems to bring us no reward at all. The only color we can see is a drab gray. We hear no music.

A haunting invitation beckons us: Drop out. Let it all go. We'll suffer no more hurt. Settle for less. Find a quiet oasis of peace. Get rid of all the anxiety and tension.

At this moment we need a lifeline. Why? Because to disappear from life is to reject it. While we're still living, that's the most self-destructive mistake we can make. A good lifeline is work. It involves us in the nitty-gritty of life, keeps us in touch with other people, provides us wonderful things called deadlines, and takes our mind off despair.

I won't give up on life till it's over.

"I work in a nursing home with elderly residents who have physical limitations and declining health. Some live with constant pain and loneliness. How can I show them that life is worth living?"

~

We always convey messages about life's meaning to others, whether we're aware of it or not. We do this simply by our attitudes, actions, and beliefs.

So, if we wish to convey the idea that life is worth living, the only real way is to believe it ourselves. Then the idea communicates itself. If we don't believe it, all efforts are doomed to failure.

It's important to realize that people who suffer pain are very, very sensitive about receiving messages. Much of the charade of life has been stripped from them. They are intuitive. With them, words are not nearly so effective as body language, attitude, and actions. Only when we believe that life is worth living can we reach out to them with that message.

I'll live as if life were worthwhile. I'll make it so.

"Even though I'm older and have had experience with panic, I just collapse when everything seems to fall apart. It makes me think of a hurricane or an earthquake."

~

Panic is a natural reaction when the roof it about to blow off or the walls cave in. We are transfixed by terror. Survival becomes our primary, immediate goal.

Emotional upheaval is just as demanding. The ground we stand on is shaking. Our support system appears to be failing. An unexpected disaster has struck. Hope seems far away. What can we do?

As soon as the wind dies down and the shaking ceases—the violent emotional eruption has lost its immediate intensity—we need to see if there is anything pragmatic and rational that we can do in the interest of survival and sanity. Then we need to center ourself, realize we're still here, and figure out what is essential to do next. The moment has come to let go of panic. Now the question is: Where do we go from here? How do we get there?

When panic threatens, I'll center myself, deal quietly and sensibly, and think about what is essential in my life.

"My grandmother has Alzheimer's disease. I just found out. I have to tell her, try to make her understand, and convince her to leave her lovely home and move into a nursing home which can take the proper care of her."

∾

A catastrophic number of older women and men have, or will develop, Alzheimer's disease.

Yet more is being learned about how to detect and treat it. An enormous mobilization of effort and funding is needed, along with ever increased public awareness, understanding, and knowledge. It is ironic that at a moment in time when AIDS strikes so many who are young, Alzheimer's strikes so many who are older. Both require top prioritization by government and health authorities.

When Alzheimer's comes into the life of someone whom we know and love, it requires all our stamina, commitment, determination, compassion, and love. No one is immune from potentially being touched by it. Alzheimer's is not an isolated disease that affects only a small number of individuals. It is universal in its scope, a health problem of the first magnitude in the ways it can reach out and affect our life.

Whatever happens to one of us, happens to all of us. I'll try to face even the worst with patience and compassion.

"Certain fears cripple me emotionally and take the vitality and joy out of living. I'm too old to have fears."

～

Fears crouch inside the various locked closets of our lives. We need to open the closet doors and bring these menacing fears into sunlight and fresh air.

President Franklin D. Roosevelt said that all we have to fear is fear itself. He was right. If we fear darkness, the best antidote is to walk into the dark and find it's safe, even comforting. If we fear another person, we need to unmask the object of our fear and speak to just another human being, not an imaginary source of terror. If we fear water, it's best to immerse our body in it, feeling its healing presence.

Life is entirely too short for us to let ourselves be crippled by irrational fears. They can take the vitality and joy out of our living. They need to be consigned to the nearest dump heap.

Today, I'll face my fears head-on. I'll render them powerless.

"I'm recovering from a stroke and had to learn how to walk, dress, and do everything for myself again. A fresh focus helped."

~

We are frequently reborn in this life. When do we experience it? In coming back to health after an illness, recovering from addiction, moving to a new location, beginning a new relationship, or undertaking a wholly new adventure.

It is remarkable that we can build a new life. It takes courage, discipline, and patience. A fresh focus is essential. It is as if we were to walk through a door, down a corridor, find a new door, discover it's not locked, open it, and walk through it into a fresh experience. Often it is an experience that is without precedent for us.

We can do this. We have enormous potential and virtually unlimited power to effect extraordinary change in our life when circumstances demand it or we will it. It's possible for us to return to square one, start over, and succeed.

There's no such thing as "too late." I'm willing to start over.

"My pain, my suffering, is burning me. I wish the strange fire might be still."

~

Pain is our universal human experience. None of us escapes it. Pain occurs in our body, in our mind, in our soul.

Trying to fight against pain is futile. It absorbs all our needed energy. Instead, we have to come to grips with it. Accept it. Let it in. Breathe with it. Move with it. Come to some kind of a truce with it. Get familiar with it. Even, on occasion, make friends with it.

Yes, we'll do everything we can to understand and treat pain's cause. There are many things we can do to alleviate it. Still, pain persists. It is a companion that stays unnaturally close to us. Once we have quit treating pain as a mortal enemy and have moved into a flexible relationship, we can begin to focus on something else. At that moment, pain can cease to be the center of our universe.

Today I'll recognize the pain, accept it, and go on to something else.

"*Forty flower bulbs were planted in my backyard. This requires three walks a day out there to see if they have surfaced. I hope you can perceive what simple crazy little things I find meaning in.*"

~

The best meaning is often found in little, simple things that can be described as very ordinary, and tend to be overlooked.

Think of the deep meaning in a family meal. Food that was grown and transported to a market has now found its way to preparation in a kitchen, and thence to a family meal. The hot bread, the roast, the vegetables and salad, and the wine await the common joy of their consumption.

Simple, crazy little things throughout our lives are the true sacraments that mark our human passage. Pretentious, big things are granted too much honor in our society. We hear about the big movie or building, corporation or church, book or salary. Meaning is frequently obliterated by bigness, which gets in the way and attracts all the attention. We need to look patiently between the cracks of life to find what rests there as a gift.

My life is full of meaning. Today, I'll find it in the unexpected places.

"I have a terminal disease and live one day at a time. I dwell on a hill, and my vegetable and flower garden is at the bottom. I get my exercise going up and down the steps."

≈

All of us must live one day at a time. But most of us don't realize it. We foolishly assume we have forever. We waste time, energy, and love.

We are all going to die. Death appears to be the only true form of democracy. Whether we arrived on the *Mayflower* or a slave ship, none of us is leaving by the first class.

Meanwhile, life beckons us. A day at a time, a step at a time, is the only plan that is really open to us. Why do we become so impatient with this? We want to leap up to reach the top of Mt. Everest without ever having learned to climb. We want to become opera stars without taking singing lessons. We hope to win a lottery, yet refuse to start a small savings account. Our worst mistake is to place our wished-for destination in life in front of us as if it were a carrot, blot out everything else, and miss the joys of the trip.

I'll respond to life today, and savor it. I won't look ahead with trepidation.

"I went into clinical depression. It was so severe I felt I was in hell. Then in my treatment, I met precious souls who did not require me to be perfect. They allowed me to be me."

∿

What an extraordinary gift you have received. You are fortunate and blessed.

Why do we so often establish perfection as a guideline for other people and ourselves? Perfectionism is a curse. No one can ever attain it. First, we set up impossible standards to reach, then we berate others and ourselves when we automatically fail.

To strive to be perfect in a family, a marriage, or any relationship is to offer the kiss of death. No one can live or breathe naturally around perfectionism. It is unyielding. And it's terrible when someone who has "failed" to be perfect is expected to ask for forgiveness. One of the most precious gifts in the whole world is to allow other people to be themselves. A further step is to love them for themselves. This means accepting their absence of perfection.

I resolve to not be perfect.

"Relaxation is the real answer to physical and emotional problems, I'm always told. Who can relax when the burdens of life are so heavy?"

~

It's exactly when the burdens of life are so heavy that we need to relax. Sadly, we make relaxation appear to be yet another heavy burden, an unsolvable problem. It isn't.

To relax means letting go of the tension in our body. (Yoga can be helpful here.) Slouch in a chair or lie on a bed. Let the shoulders drop. Breathe deeply and consciously—in and out, in and out. Sustain the breathing. Relax a finger, then a hand, then an arm. Relax a toe, then a foot, then a leg. Imagine floating.

To relax also means letting go of the tension in our mind. If there is an obsessive and heavy thought or problem, turn away from it for a moment. Focus elsewhere. See a fountain, an ocean, a lake, a valley. A dog, a cat, a horse, a fish. Bright yellow, burnt orange, turquoise, sea blue, red, white, black, mauve, a pine tree, a rose bush. A city street, a country road, a building, people walking, people running, people surfing. Think of something light or beautiful or uplifting.

I'll focus on hope and love. For a day, I'll relax.

"I have learned to take pain in small segments. I will get through the next half-hour. Then, the next."

～

There's only so much we can take at a time. When we attempt to look out over the vast span of our lives, we are mystified, immobilized.

Yet if we can differentiate between portions of the immense vista of life, and endeavor to cope only with a workable part of it, perhaps we can manage effectively. Pain is unlike anything else. It makes extraordinary demands on us. Too, it becomes familiar. We grow accustomed to when it comes, when it goes. Imagining and anticipating a full span of uninterrupted pain can be devastating. We need to yield and deal pragmatically with pain on our own terms in whatever ways we can.

Life itself is a bit like pain in this regard. We can't take it in one fell swoop, nor are we asked to. Yet, in segments, we find that we gradually learn how to manage it when its sharp sensations are balanced by quiet nurturing, its pains with celebrations of joy.

I won't look at life simply as a whole, but as a wonderful collection of fragments.

"I'm old and physically helpless. I can't tie my shoes or feed myself. But I can visit a nursing home and talk to a friend who is in worse shape than I am."

～

In a world that sadly needs far more of them, we need all the stories we can find about human generosity and kindness.

When we reach out and help someone else, we're not only helping them. We're helping ourselves, too. We are becoming better persons. Our vistas grow wider instead of narrower. Self-interest makes room for interest beyond the self. Kindness is taking concrete form somewhere in the universe at this moment. Generosity becomes more than just a slogan, it is being practiced right now.

Some people ask, "Where can I find someone else who is in serious need of help?" Walk a city block among the homeless. Listen to people who are hungry. See loneliness a few seats away. Be aware of what people are not saying in their well-chosen, careful, often frightened words. These are the words of loved ones, friends, acquaintances, and strangers. Needs are all about us. We can commence by responding to one. Then, another. And another.

I'll leave off my own worries for a day. I'll try my hand at affecting another's life.

"I look awful, feel exhausted all the time, and am so lonely I could go bonkers. I can't turn my life around or go anywhere. Unless the heavens open up with miracles pouring down like rain, it looks hopeless for me."

～

A number of us feel this way on occasion. We lose perspective momentarily. We forget how really great we are. So we stop taking good care of ourselves, give in to misery, and accept a jury's negative verdict.

Yet there is neither a jury nor a verdict. Instead, there is only our own lack of confidence, absence of hope, and denial of the reality of goodness. Feeling sunk at certain moments is a universal experience. However, we're not sunk unless we believe we are.

Certainly, we cannot totally change our lives as if by magic. Yet we can make daily, significant changes. We can start healing depression, get rest or a new spark if we're tired out, reach out to others if we're lonely, fix up the way we look, get something to wear—and find a mirror, look into it, and smile. The message is: We can change *can't* to *want*.

What sort of miracle would it take to make me happy? Today, I'll picture that miracle. Then, I'll begin moving toward it.

❦ Changes ❦

"My mother's drinking problem got worse and worse. She was an alcoholic when my husband died unexpectedly three years ago. I desperately needed her wisdom and help. Almost as if by a miracle, my mother stopped drinking, and her support made all the difference in my life."

∼

We tend to forget how closely interwoven our life is with the lives of others, especially loved ones and close friends.

A tremendous challenge arises for us when someone close is in terrible trouble or faces a life crisis. It can bring out the best in us when we attempt to offer help and everything we can, at the cost of our own convenience and resources.

At such a moment we may rise to levels of maturity beyond our comprehension. While helping someone else, we've been helped immeasurably by our acts of generosity that were not rooted in self-interest. A call for help can cut through tangled emotions and bring out the best in our human spirit.

Miracles have to start somewhere. Today, I'll answer a call for help.

"My lover and I broke up four years ago and I've been living alone. I'm a sixty-seven-year-old lesbian and a successful businesswoman who has a workaholic streak. Recently I met another woman who loves me and has asked to make a life with me. But I'm afraid. I don't know if I dare risk a new relationship."

~

One of the worst mistakes we can ever make is to give up on life.

The energy and momentum of life is one of its greatest surprises. To cooperate with it is important. This is an acknowledgment of its power and potential for us. There are times when life itself seems to have a plan for us, surpassing anything we can dream up. Our positive response is needed.

If we mistrust possibility, deny the lovely meaning of serendipity in our life, and announce our best days and years are behind us, we put up roadblocks. We don't need them! They get in the way of everything. Better to let the way ahead lie open and unhindered. Then we can dare, and take a risk. We can even believe it's not a risk at all.

I won't hang back from opportunity because of age. I'm alive, and I deserve to go on *living*.

"For thirty years my husband and I lived for each other alone. 'Let's shut out the world,' he'd always say, drawing the blinds. Now, without him, I'm finding it's not so easy to let the world back in."

≈

It takes a fine balancing act to draw satisfaction and enjoyment from our personal life and, at the same time, to honor and serve the world around us.

Ultimately, they don't represent an either/or choice at all. Unless we live in the world actively, we deny ourself the full meaning of a rich life. If we don't put aside time and energy for a full personal life, we can easily become embittered and end up not having a whole life at all.

The secret seems to be sharing our personal life, not hoarding it for ourself. When two people attempt to exist in isolation, they commit a fatal error. Personal life needs to be opened up to include the world. This doesn't mean all of it rushing in in one fell swoop, but entering gradually, wisely, richly.

Today, I step down off the funeral pyre.

"My husband is a workaholic. He's sixty-eight and seems to think he's twenty-eight, judging by the hours he works and the stress he's under. He keeps talking about the likelihood he'll die first and I will be a widow. I wish I could pick him up by the nape of his neck and get him out of his damned office."

~

We can't teach an old dog new tricks. Nor can we provide a new scenario for another person's existence.

So, when confronted by a characteristic or a trait in another person that's driving us crazy, we have at least two choices. We can make it to the center of our life, allowing it to become an obsessive cause of anxiety. Or, we can realize it is out of our capacity to change it. Then we place it on the periphery of our life, readjust our priorities, and no longer let it drive us nuts.

When we can't change someone else or difficult circumstances, we can change ourself and the way we look at a problem. We should never let it dominate our thinking, our feelings, our perspective—our life.

I cannot change another. Only myself. Today, I'll work to change my own perspective on an old problem.

"My wife and I were married for thirty-two years when she said she didn't love me anymore. She rejected me and wanted to live alone. I was stunned. I lost my self-respect. I moved out, left her the house, rented a small walk-up apartment, divided our savings with her. We have no children. Now I am without companionship or love and have nothing to live for."

~

Life can sometimes resemble the *Titanic*. When the proud, seemingly secure ocean liner hit an iceberg in the mid-Atlantic, it sank. There are moments when we seem to be sinking, too.

We can be surprised by what life brings us! Despair and a sense of terrible loss are often first reactions. But we don't have the luxury of time for these if our ship is sinking in icy water amid raging waves. We've got to find a lifeboat and make our way to safety and survival.

The instinct to go on living is our best ally in terms of adversity. It pumps adrenalin, keeps our mind alert, and makes us realize we face a truly awesome challenge. We have no time to indulge feelings of self-pity. We've got to fight against adversity and get our life back.

I'm ready for any challenge. I have survived adversity before, and I can do it again.

"Our three children are grown and married, but they still rely on my husband and me to be their parents as if they were helpless kids. We're sick of the whole thing and want to live our old age out happily. Why don't they grow up? Why don't they treat us with gratitude for all we've done for them?"

~

All of us are conditioned by numerous forces to see primary people in our life in terms of patriarchal and matriarchal roles.

A mother is *a mother*, not simply a close friend or a loved one. A father is *a father*. These roles carry a lot of hereditary and emotional luggage.

A mother, then, is supposed to act like *a mother*; this can severely limit her freedom to be herself. A father is similarly fenced in, facing the same kind of limitations. It can take years for a child to reach a place of enough maturity and freedom to be able in turn to grant freedom to parents to be *themselves*.

Today, I give myself and others a clean slate. I'll try responding without old expectations. I'll provide novelty.

"Twenty-six years ago I was virtually at the end of my rope, lost in a sea of alcoholism. Now I am in recovery."

～

At particular moments life can seem hopeless. Apparently (we feel) there is no light at the end of the tunnel. We seem to have lost everything. We're hurt and embarrassed, and it seems we've given up.

It is precisely at such moments that the great turning points in our life may occur. We discern a semblance of light at the faraway end of an unimaginably dark tunnel. We catch a glimmer of hope, are touched by a spark of understanding.

Aliveness intervenes, and we're a bit like Lazarus walking outside his tomb. Everything has not been solved. Much work remains to be done. Transformation will absorb countless hours, days, and years of our life, a step at a time. Yet peace exists where it did not. The sun has come out. It feels good to be alive.

Today, I congratulate myself for the changes I've made. I recognize the job continues.

"I'm a healthy, active seventy-five-year-old lady born with-out direction finders. I'm looking for a strong old man to go mountain hiking with me because I get lost alone, hate snakes, and can't keep my food out of the reach of bears."

$\sim$

All of us need to do more mountain hiking or an equivalent, get out in the wilds, sight a grizzly, and encounter a long, colorful snake. Our lives become too safe, too predictable, too tame. However, what we really want is to climb life's mountains and hills without direction finders at all.

Most of the time we know exactly where we're going in the morning, at noon, and at night. Our travel route is as predict-able as a sunset. There's no question about whom we will see, or where, or why. There are no risks on the horizon. No strangers. Our lives become as cut-and-dried as if they had been sitting out on the kitchen sink. Let's throw away direction finders and go hiking in a real wilderness.

I'm ready to start fresh. I'll step into the wilderness and follow my instincts.

"I'm a fifty-eight-year-old gay man. My life-partner died two years ago. I live alone in the home we shared. Despite having lots of friends, staying exceptionally active, and holding down a responsible managerial position that keeps me unusually busy, I am desperately lonely and worry about what the future holds."

~

It can be a mistake when we keep running too fast and too hard after we've suffered loss and pain.

At times it's necessary to slow down, accept the solace and deep meaning of solitude, and cultivate patience. This can prove to be very healing.

We can be on a perpetual merry-go-round, with noise and distraction, lots of activism and socializing, yet lose contact with the center of our own life. The center is indispensable for our spiritual and emotional renewal. When we're in close touch with it, we can deal much better with loss and loneliness, and quietly peer at our future with patience.

I won't be afraid of solitude. Today, I'll quit running away and give loss my full attention.

"I'll be damned if I'll go around making monkey faces and kissing babies just because I'm old enough to be a grand-mother. If they're interested, they can come kiss me."

～

Sometimes we find we've overextended ourself and gone out to the world altogether too much. It's time to pause, change our rhythm, and let the world come to us for a change. Then a new balance can emerge.

Maybe it's time to surprise others who live or work with us by asserting a new side of our personality they aren't accustomed to. They can meet a part of us that deserves attention, space, time, oxygen, love—and applause. All this can take place in a new scenario of our life that we introduce.

Change is not only beneficial, but downright necessary on occasion. If we've gone out of our way to please others too much, perhaps we want to less now to win their favor and instead ask them to support us in a fresh mood. Or, if we've been self-centered and refused to please others, maybe the moment has come to be more outgoing, generous, sacrificing, and loving.

I won't let my behavior be dictated by age.

"I've found a lot of my life to be tough as nails, unreward-ing, and —in my opinion—unfair. At the same time people (including my family, people in religion, and therapists I've used) tell me to have hope and be 'positive.' Why should I? How can I?"

~

The best part of our life may be just around the next corner.

It's crucial that we retain our belief in this. Life thrusts us forward. The best part need not be buried in memories. Our validation should not be sought in former successes, joys, achievements, and friendships. In its mysterious and fascinat-ing ways, life summons us to move ahead and discover ever new treasures of the spirit.

How can we live fully in hope, in love, and with faith? By taking risks. By continuing to grow as a person, never rest-ing on past laurels. In order to claim our wholeness we must dare. We need to define what we have lacked up to now, what we want that we don't have, and what it will take to make us whole. This means being truly alive. This means being open to what we do not yet know.

I'll embrace life fully every day, with all the wisdom of my years, and all the innocence of a child. I'll begin *now*.

"For fifty years I lived happily with another woman. Now she's dead, I'm eighty years old and scared. My nurse has brought me back to the church and made me give up all my 'evil' friends. Now I'm lonely."

~

We have to assert our independence again and again, remaining ever vigilant. There everlastingly seems to be somebody waiting in the wings to keep us from being free.

There are zealots who vociferously declaim they're limiting our freedom for our own good. Why they wish to become self-appointed arbiters of public morality remains a puzzle. Perhaps they were bitterly unhappy in their childhood, and want everyone else to share their misery. They seem to hurt badly when they see a happy face; they don't want anyone to fly. They cast imprecations to bring others down to a level where they can seize their joy.

It's up to us to assert our rights against such misguided, dictatorial zealots. No one has any right to scare us and make us feel lonely or hopeless. No one.

I won't let fear or prejudice narrow my life—not mine, not anyone else's.

"My life was my husband and family. He was diagnosed with lung cancer and in a year he was dead and I felt part of me had died."

∾

We love to have a sense of structure in our life. It can seem like the Rock of Gibraltar, absolutely sage and unassailable.

But the structure can come apart, fall down, and change completely before our eyes. There is never any guaranteed permanence in human life. A death or illness, accident or an unexpected disaster, can topple what appeared to be our security.

When our life changes abruptly, we must be resilient, accept the fact, and get on with living as well as possible. Maybe we'll feel we're not the same person we were because the entire content of our life has been irremediably changed. What is new, even if we can't recognize it yet, is all we have. We must manage to create a new life.

The only surety in life is change. I'll embrace it. I'm still alive.

"Mothers try so hard to be included with their daughters, and it's a losing battle."

~

The whole meaning of a family is undergoing radical change. One out of three American children is growing up with one parent. Children receive primary instruction from their peers and mass media.

In older days, the family was far more self-contained. Elderly members often lived as integral parts of the family. There could be natural interaction between young and old members.

Lots of working fathers and mothers now have little opportunity to spend much time with their children. Everybody can seem to be on an assembly-line schedule. Slack time is frequently filled by TV. Communication grows harder, not easier. It seems an excellent idea whenever mothers can spend time with daughters, fathers with sons, mothers with sons, fathers with daughters. It's sad when people in a family have to remain strangers, alienated, unable to know one another.

I accept the changing roles in my family. I'll strive to be friend foremost, brother, mother, cousin second.

"I have never married and have never been an outgoing person. After my mother's death I looked after my father for twenty-one years until he died when I was sixty-three. I am determined to make the most of what is left of my life."

∽

Each of our lives is an incredible mystery. Each tells its own story, weaves its unique pattern, conjures up a set of different meanings.

None of our lives reveals its deepest truths on the surface. We make the mistake sometimes of pitying someone who has no need of pity, or rewarding someone who deserves no reward. We're working in the dark here. Using outward symbols reflected by a life, we make assumptions and act upon them.

I think the most important thing to do with any life is make the most of what's left. This brings us strongly into the present moment. What's past is gone. The future we do not know. But in the present moment we can harness our energy, gather up our dreams, and aim to make the very most of what remains. While this may sound like an awesome task, it's a realizable one.

Today, I'll ponder the rest of my story. I'll consider where I'd like the plot to turn. Then, I'll begin to make it happen.

"There must be a man who would enjoy the company of a fifty-one-year-old woman who has to make it happen again. There must be more to life than to sit it out alone."

~

We can't wait, any of us, for good things to happen in our life. It is a passive attitude that can stand in the way of anything happening.

We've got to be willing to initiate action. Get out there and connect with somebody and make it happen. If there's a job we want, it won't do any good to sit quietly and hope it will come to us. It won't. It can't. We've got to go after it, say we want it, plan on it, talk to people about it.

The same thing is true of a relationship. Waiting alone, wistfully yearning for lightning to strike in the guise of Mr. Right or Ms. Right marching into our life while the band plays, is guaranteed to keep it from occurring. We have to define what we want, make plans, and go for it.

I refuse to sit this out alone. I'll initiate action.

"After a lifetime of giving, it is now my turn to receive. My family will grow in the process as I find a new life, one more devoted to my own welfare."

～

Reciprocity is fairness. No one person should give and give and give, and not receive, while another receives and receives and receives.

We've all known an unappreciated giver. Other givers allow an imbalance to grown between their giving and receiving. This can be near fatal. However, an unappreciated giver should not be required to bear the additional burden of asking for a change. Since we're dealing here with a dysfunctional situation, this often happens.

When a change is requested, it may come as a shock to an insensitive receiver who has blatantly exploited the role of a giver. Yet such a moment of truth is significant for both a receiver and a giver. The time has come for someone else's turn. Now a giver can experience what it feels like to be a receiver.

Today, I'll ask for my fair share.

"Six years ago I buried my twenty-five-year-old son who desperately wanted to live. Now my eighty-year-old mother is causing me stress, havoc, and much anguish because she wants to die. I can't find any justice or peace in this."

～

Life holds a mixed bag of surprises, as we all know. Often we cannot find any justice in our situation. However, it's up to us to find peace.

It's heartbreaking when someone we love, who adores life and lives it to the hilt, perishes in an accident or dies slowly of an incurable disease. It's agonizing when someone we love, who has pulled back from the dynamic of life and wishes fervently to die, lives on and on in excruciating pain or emotional despair.

The dilemma, in all its irony, lies outside the bailiwick of our power to change it. Our attitude, however, is up to us. We can't wish reality away. We have to accept it, decide we won't let it destroy our life, and find peace in acceptance.

Today, I'll acknowledge the unpredictability of life. I'll accept what I can't change, and work on what I can. I'll look for peace in acceptance.

"I am caught in the sandwich generation between my children (whom I have lost all patience with) and my mother (who is absolutely impossible). I am fifty-seven. I thought these years would be my happiest. Help!"

∾

If you had thought you could simply retire and go fishing, you were dead wrong. You'll need all the help you can get.

The demands made upon people who are caught between their responsibilities toward children and parents are sometimes awesome. A basic rule is: Don't lose patience. It is a prerequisite for survival.

While we need to cultivate patience within ourselves, there is another need, too. It is to feel patience toward other people in our lives who can't help the fact that they are problems for us. They can never be regarded as absolutely impossible. A far better attitude is *always possible*. We must remain open to a full range of possibility when it comes to the other key players in our life. Remember: Our present years can be our happiest—but only if we make them that way.

My happiness is up to me. Today, I'll work with reality, but look for possibilities.

"I am a gay man of seventy-four. My partner died of a heart attack several years ago and unless I find someone else I love as much, he will not be replaced. I keep busy playing music and composing."

~

None of us ever knows our life may be changed by something that happens. It is necessary to make our peace with the givenness of life: a death, a separation, an ending.

At the same time, it is vital that we do not place a bolt on a closed door of our life. We may later wish to open the door again; it may simply be opened for us. To make up our mind with finality that there is no new possibility waiting for us is a mistake, because it can appear without warning at any time.

When a door has closed for us, and no new possibility has revealed itself, keeping busy helps make us flexible and saves us from fixating on a painful loss. Busyness is not enough, however. We should strive to maintain openness to serendipity, chance, and possibility. It's good for us to be ready for changes whenever they make an appearance on our doorstep.

There will be endings in my life. But there will always be beginnings. I embrace both.

"After forty-two years of marriage, the situation just became such that I could not live with it anymore. I moved out of our home, rented a small apartment, continued with the job I love, and have made a very happy life for myself."

~

Sometimes decisions loom on the horizon like a tidal wave. They force themselves upon us.

Some are complex and hard. We end a relationship, leave a profession or job, move to a new place where we don't know a soul. Wouldn't it be easier to be placed on the rack? Our happiness and well-being seem threatened. We're risking everything with no reward at all in sight. Looking at our window, the view is bleak; it's icy and cold and we're scared to death.

However, we may find happiness beyond our imagination once we've made a clear decision, taken risks in stride, and moved forward. We can't know until we do it. Our attitude is very important. Just to stand still is out of the question, anyway, because we're changing all the time. So is everyone and everything else.

I won't be afraid to make a move. I'll consider my decision, and then I'll stride ahead.

"*Older people have seen too much, been through too much, to be surprised by anything.*"

~

After we've lived many years, it's obvious that we've seen and experienced a great deal of life. Are there any surprises left?

Yes fortunately, they never end. We can be surprised by a wide assortment of things including rain, sunshine, betrayal, trust, hate, love, new neighbors, old neighbors, loud noise, a movie, a book, taxes, and death. Surprises provide zest and dash to living. They mean that we're never able to take anything for granted.

It seems to me, in fact, that the older we get, the more surprises there are. Presumably, we've grown so sophisticated and knowledgeable about life, we shouldn't be surprised by anything anymore. But we are. Oh, we are.

Today, I'll welcome a surprise. It's essential to being alive.

"I want to keep trying, take risks, keep going, experiment with life, undertake new ventures, and find fresh challenges."

∿

As long as we have breath we can move forward. There is a certain possibility for each of us.

We dare not be self-destructive by giving up. Life is beautiful, a splendid mystery that is our gift. Each day is a new day. To live fully implies that we keep trying. Trying to do what? To choose joy, perceive beauty, reach out, be opened to possibility rather than closed to it, and expect love—even in the face of indifference or hate.

It is exciting to take risks. They open up new windows and doors in our lives, bearing us outside our secret, locked rooms. It is an utterly beneficial thing to experiment with life and play with fresh variations. The lure of something new and original lies just around the next corner. Turn the corner. Accept a fresh challenge.

Today I'll try something totally different. I'll take an unexpected risk. I'll play with fresh variations.

"*I am retired, make do with a small pension and social security, and am writing a novel, making quilts, sewing, knitting, reading, listening to music, going places, and my life is great.*"

~

One of the greatest blessings is finding what we like to do, and doing it. There is nothing worse than doing day by day what we detest and find utterly boring and meaningless.

This holds true in all our lives, whether we're poor or rich, rural or urban, retired or in the workplace. It's really up to us, as individuals, to choose what sense we can make out of life. Opportunity is wide open. Someone holding down an eight-hour job can manage to have hobbies or volunteer in a neighborhood activity, pursue a personal goal or continue an education.

After retirement, it's entirely possible to open up a whole new world of creativity, challenge, and interest. In this case, "retirement" becomes something of a misnomer. A wealth of potential awaits us when we decide to seek new adventure, fresh goals, and maybe even an undiscovered continent we never dreamed of.

What is that I really want to do? Why am I not doing it? Today, I'm going to set a goal and start toward it.

"I'm not doing what I want to do with the precious time I have left."

~

In certain moments of unusual clarity we are able to see ourselves, and our lives, in a sudden shock of recognition.

We can see what is good and what is lacking. When we're conscious of the shortness of remaining time, it's possible for us to make significant decisions. For example, if something makes us unhappy, we can change it or remove it from our life. If something else represents an agony or a failure for us, we can refuse to let it block our view of wholeness.

The precious time we have left assumes major importance. In terms of decision making, it is a question of now or never. The actress Gloria Swanson wisely noted that never is a long, undependable time, and life is too full of rich possibilities to have restrictions placed on it. *Now* is a much more positive and energizing word than *never*, which is negative, imprisoning, stultifying, and reproaches our possibilities. We need to decide now to do what we want with the time we have.

I'm going to cut the word *never* out of my vocabulary, and make *now* the thrust of my life.

"There's no way out."

≈

Life is constructed as a medieval fortress. It is a vast, intricate network, with infinite and subtle connections. It's important to remember that there's always a way in and a way out.

When we're confronted by seemingly insurmountable problems, it's easy to feel claustrophobic and shut in. The walls seem to be pressing ever closer. There is no window to see through. No doorway appears as a possible exit. It seems that we are a victim like the tragic figure in Edgar Allen Poe's *The Pit and the Pendulum,* who cannot escape a terrible fate, and even has to watch as it approaches.

This is precisely the moment when we need to visualize an alternative of liberation. We see beyond the threatening walls that seem ready to crush us. We see through the monstrous weight poised to destroy us. Now a way out appears. We see we're in a fluid situation, with lots of openings.

I'll open a window. I'll step through a doorway. I'll find an opening today.

"My ritual of sameness, day after day, makes me feel simply numb. Can I change?"

≈

It's so easy for us to get locked inside a routine that seems to take over our life. Why do we let it?

There are innumerable ways to vary an existing routine, but they require our imagination and effort. All sorts of routines mark the maps of our daily lives. Going to work, going shopping, washing dishes, washing clothes, preparing meals, eating meals, watching TV, paying bills, putting out the garbage. On and on.

Driving to work, it's possible to discover an interesting new route. This lets us look at different streets, trees, buildings, billboards, and whatever comes into view. This is a small thing, but life is made up of small things. Or, take lunch. We don't have to go with the same people to the same place and have the same conversation. We can go for a walk. Locate a quiet spot and read. Eat an apple. You see? It's up to us. When we change small things, big things follow.

I'll try something totally out of character today. I'll dabble with change, and await the results.

"As I grow older, younger people help me stay in touch with new ideas by occasionally shocking the hell out of me."

~

There is always something that's even newer than what's new. We live on the edge of continuing discoveries, revelations, and creations.

What's new does not always come from someone who is young. But the adage that the young see visions while the old dream dreams holds a lot of truth. Older people had an earlier chance to see visions, wrestle with their meanings, and contribute ideas that probably shocked their elders at the time.

When a newer generation appears, inevitably there are new styles, expressions of personal identity, causes of social justice, and forms of behavior. Some of these have past counterparts, others do not. Shock value can be extremely helpful when it enables us to focus on a problem in an altogether different way, and see alternatives and possibilities we could not even imagine before.

I resolve to be open to what's new and different, even when it "shocks" me.

"This moment is of supreme importance. In another moment it will be gone. Can I hold onto it?"

~

No. We cannot place time inside a jar as if it were honey. Time is like the air. It brushes against our face and is gone forever.

It is important that we honor each moment as it comes. Acknowledge it fully. Take delight in it as we may. Recognize the sacred quality of time, its transient nature, its extraordinary beauty as a sheer gift.

Almost as soon as it came, the moment is gone, replaced with another one. The moments multiply and make an hour, a day, a week, a month, a year, a life. We can learn the art of gracefully letting a moment go when it is ready, offering thanks for it, anticipating its successor. This means being open to the precious gift of the moment, realizing its import. While seasons return, moments do not.

I won't cling to the moment. I'll set it free—making room for the next one.

"I realize I am not going to live forever. Can I handle this?"

≈

You'd better. Maybe sooner rather than later.

Of course there is widespread and deep belief in numerous religions and spiritual resources that the soul, or personality, continues after the death of the body.

But in this moment let's deal simply with the here and now. Yes, a lot of people fear death. Yet it seems a logical, clean-cut climax to our earthly existence. It's hard for most of us to spend a great deal of time on life's joys and issues, problems and possibilities. It seems necessary to concentrate on the next immediate steps of this life instead of speculating about what comes afterward. At the same time, we've got to be prepared for the end of our lives—make our wishes known concerning our possessions, remember loved ones and friends, and develop a state of mind that contains readiness for our inevitable demise. Live fully—but leave some space for what is to come.

I'll recognize the inevitability of an ending—consider what's necessary—and then stride straight ahead into the future.

"Was this what it came to—that you could never escape?"

~

We have to believe that we can make changes in our lives. Otherwise we become victims.

Possessing the power to make changes, however, does not in any way free us from the need to confront life's demands. We can't rub a genie's lamp, make three wishes, and have them magically granted. It's necessary to work our way through problems. The point is: We can make the fastest progress by expeditiously tackling the rough terrain one step at a time.

The really hard question is: Is there escape from aging? No—but there is escape from negative thinking about it. We can be grateful for the positive gifts of growing more mature, finally coming to see the whole of life in perspective, and reaching a coveted and golden place of wisdom.

I'll focus today on gratitude. I'm grateful for change, and the chance for something new.

"*I am divorced, poor, out of work and insurance, and my dreams are crushed by bankers. At fifty-seven, it is hard to keep dreaming.*"

~

But you must. Without your dreams, what have you got?

We must never let ourselves become trapped within a negative vision of life. We are not meant to be victims. *Victim* is a bad word. We can reject it, with all its connotations of helplessness and despair.

Possibility is always ahead of us as long as we are breathing. Victimization is a self-perpetuating exercise in futility. It is a vicious cycle and leads nowhere except to more of the same. Some of us feel at times: "I am a throwaway." "My dreams are crushed." "I am out of everything I need." These require responses. Only we can make the responses. "I am not a throwaway." "My dreams cannot be crushed." "It's time to let the past be the past, and I will find new needs." Our dreams need to be understood as parts of The Dream. It is about liberation and fulfillment. The Dream tells us unequivocally that we can start over.

My life starts today. I'm starting to dream.

"Retirement is simply another form of challenge, but a delightful one because for once I get to make the rules. I get to decide just how fulfilling or empty by life will be."

∾

Isn't it wonderful to be able to make a choice? Imagine we're in a forest, night is falling, and our path suddenly breaks into two different directions. Which one to take? The decision is terribly important and could be a life-or-death choice.

So is our choice about whether our life will be empty or fulfilling. This is our choice. An empty life is a selfish one. It exists when we shut out the rest of the world, creating a tiny semblance of a universe that caters exclusively to what we assume are our needs. A fulfilling life, on the other hand, is a shared one. We relate to different people, offer help, listen, and practice what's called empathy. The rules are finally up to us. There is no longer any authority figure telling us what to do, or even offering suggestions.

Retirement is an enormous challenge—and opportunity. We may become active in ways we never imagined, and also allow time for creative solitude. Why not occasionally sit under a friendly tree and meditate like the saints?

Today, I'll think about my choices. And then I'll choose.

"I had a real crisis at sixty. All my life I'd been active—worked, raised a family. Suddenly everything came to a dead halt. I ran out of energy and hope, and hated my life. Now, thank God, I am back on track. I'm taking an aerobics class, studying Spanish, and feel alive and happy to greet the new day. It's marvelous."

∾

Life goes on and gets better when it is treated with affection, good sense, and obdurate determination.

Our opportunities for living richly and more fully are legion. Studying a foreign language, for example, is immensely helpful not only when visiting the land of its origin, but also for training the mind to remember. A class that involves the body physically—aerobics, dance, exercise, yoga—tunes up one's whole being.

These are the sort of things we should pursue at all ages and stages of our lives. It's as important in our thirties and forties as in our seventies. Sometimes we need a push or shove to get started in a new program for our mind and body. A challenge from a friend can be helpful. So can a firm resolution, and following through.

Life goes on. Today, I resolve to go with it.

~ Wisdom ~

"I'm sixty-five, a woman who is alone, and I work in the realty business. I work my butt off, and love every minute of it. People keep asking me when I'm going to retire. Why should I? I think they'll have to carry me off."

~

One person's cup of tea is another person's gin martini or chocolate milkshake.

We like different things. Our tastes vary widely. So do our ambitions and goals. For example, one person genuinely wishes to retire at the earliest opportunity in order to develop new interests or even do nothing at all. Another person can't bear the idea of retiring, loves his or her work, and just keeps rolling along.

We should never try to force our view upon someone else's life. If a person wants to work until he or she drops, we can be supportive. If a person wishes to bail out and cease work as quickly as possible, we can be helpful. Rule one: If someone wants a cup of Earl Grey tea, don't serve a cup of espresso.

There's no one to measure myself against, no expectations to meet but my own. I'm moving straight ahead, on my own path.

"I've got lots of time on my hands. One thing I do is build little monuments on my front lawn. I made a sculpture out of an old birdhouse, my old motorcycle goggles, and a bunch of model plane wings. People probably think I'm nuts."

~

One of the best things in life is to be creative. Another is to be ourself, unself-consciously and honestly.

It's sad when we don't express ourself, show our real feelings, or have the guts to do creative things because we fear others may laugh at us and fail to understand what we're doing.

If they don't get the point, it's their loss—not ours, unless we make the fatal error of worrying about what they'll say about us. Once we start doing that, there's no end to our dilemma. We can't ever please everybody else. We will never be fully accepted and understood by everybody. Some will understand us and *not* accept us. The beginning of wisdom is to accept ourself and give full rein to any forms of creativity that might grow out of us.

I'll nurture my creative impulse as I would a threatened species. I won't be curtailed by images or opinions.

"I have worked hard all my life. I thought old age would mean I was finally free to enjoy my life. But I find my children's lives are coming apart. My son just got divorced after twenty-six years of marriage. My daughter's life is in shambles—bad husband, unemployment, sick kids. I wish I could live my life instead of theirs."

∾

It's said we come into the world alone and depart it the same way.

There is, in any case, an awareness of our own identity. We are not simply a daughter, a son, a mother, a father, a wife, a husband, a sister, a brother, a boss, an employee, a neighbor, a youth, an elder. We are highly individual persons as well as incredibly unique women and men.

A corollary is that we have our own life to live. We can't live anyone else's. No one else can live ours. It can be a splendid thing to sacrifice for others and give, give, give. Yet we need to receive as well as to give. If we don't respect our life, how can we respect anyone else's? We have to live our own life instead of the lives of others.

Today, I'll focus on living my own life. I won't attempt to live the lives of others.

"Sitting in a dark room never solves anything."

~

Whenever we can, it's good to let the sunlight in. We can see more clearly. Usually we feel better.

Life requires light and movement. Life is an ongoing enterprise. It has a beginning, a middle, and an end. The end conveys a sense of destination and purpose.

Life involves other people. It's not good to become reclusive and isolated. There are difficult moments when we simply run out of fuel, and need someone to walk in and give us a mighty shove. However, we can't count on that. We may have to become a self-starter. This requires our making a decision, screwing up our courage, and making a real move. Don't forget, it's easier to do this in a sunlit room than a dark one.

I don't have time to brood. Today, I head for the light and open air.

"An older person in a state of true contentment is to be envied beyond all others."

~

There is something indescribably beautiful about a life near completion that is incandescent and shines bright. We can see in the eyes of such a person innocence and maturity, awareness and forgiveness. It's almost as if the life were exposed as, say the trunk of a giant redwood tree, it's course marked by cylindrical cycles.

To be in the presence of such a person seems a blessing. Each word, every gesture, holds meanings. There are mysteries to be unraveled here, secrets told, wisdom extracted. Time seems to stand still or else move very, very slowly; it is no longer in control. Silences communicate volumes. Fully here, we're also in another country, another realm. We feel life itself is about to be explained after the next breath, the next moment.

Whom would I consider my elders? Today, I'm going to look out for contentment in someone older. I'll think about what would bring contentment in my life.

"The seasons of the year speed by and I try to catch up with them in my own life, and usually don't succeed. I wish I could understand the lessons they might teach me as I struggle day by day."

~

We have inner seasons as well as outer ones. The two often converge.

In a cold winter we can be like a bear in a cave, hibernating, staying warm, gathering energy. Perhaps we're an introspective bear. In spring a long, long anticipation gives way to freshness and lightness and brightness and stirrings of ecstasy. In summer we can laze by the meandering river, take the boat out on the water, nap beneath a leafy tree, walk deep into the forest, then sit in a hammock and read a thick book.

Autumn is the most mysterious of the seasons. We feel it deep in our soul. There's a bracing wind, red leaves fall, we seem to be waiting for something to come. Mortality is in the air, along with wisdom and discipline and a different quality of light.

This is my season. Today I'll take a walk through fallen leaves, and think about what's ending, and what's beginning, in my life.

"It's such a mistake to waste time. It's more valuable than gold and diamonds and money."

∽

Wasting time is wasting life. Yet what does it mean to waste it?

Workaholics want to account for every moment, every hour. They believe in keeping busy and working hard. Some may consider it a waste to wander by a seashore, smell a rose, visit an art museum (unless as part of a school course), stop to watch a fountain cascade, or sit around and sing songs.

It isn't. Time exists for us. We don't exist for time. It's up to us what we want to do with it. Some perceive time as if it were a formidable mountain to be climbed, and they treat it aggressively and competitively. Others may see it as a rambling, gently moving stream, and treat it amiably and kindly. How we see time says more about us than it does about time. We should make it a friend, not an enemy. It's not a bad idea to love time.

How am I spending my "valuables"? Today, I'm going to give myself a gift of time, and do something just because I chose to.

"I am one of those unfulfilled souls who feels life has passed me by. Deep inside we feel like sad cases of life run aground, left out of the mainstream."

～

We need to define life for ourself, not accept abstract definitions given us by others. Any judgment about our fulfillment, or lack of it, needs to be correlated with how we define it.

Some people feel they're in the mainstream, others don't. What is the mainstream? It depends on one's point of view. This leads to enormous confusion when we start to measure ourselves according to other people's standards.

Comparing ourself with others can lead to deep trouble. Compared to so-and-so, we may appear unfulfilled. But, lacking that comparison, we're not! Again, a comparison with someone may give the impression our life has run aground. We need to avoid foolish comparisons and define our own fulfillment, our own concept of what's mainstream.

Today, I won't weigh my life against the mainstream. I'll think about value in my own currency.

"I can't drive a nail, put a screw in properly, or do anything that requires carpentry. This is tough when I need to put up curtain rods."

~

We can't, any of us, do everything. We need help. When we share our skills, the necessary work gets done.

It's no longer even fashionable to be omnipotent. Our world is too complicated, divided into all kinds of areas of expertise. Law and medicine are riddles with specialists. It's increasingly hard for us even to be an expert in a single field; it rapidly becomes subdivided.

An essential element of survival is knowing when to shout "Help!" Everybody does it. It holds no shame. And it provides someone else a chance to do something. Self-reliance was fine on the frontier, but it's outmoded today. It's impossible given the complexity of our shared life. We need to learn how to do our thing, let other people do theirs. The age of solitary heroes and heroines is rapidly vanishing. Group action has taken over.

I'll focus on what I know. And I won't be afraid to ask for help.

"Another day has passed so quickly. I am growing older, and it scares me."

~

When we're young, often we want to grow older. When we're older, often we would like to grow younger.

We're not easily satisfied. The grass always seems to be greener on the other side of the fence. In youth we yearn for more maturity and experience, and to become wiser in the ways of the world. But in older age we can miss the zest of youth, the sheer energy that accompanies it, along with an innocence of spirit and an untested optimism.

It's best for us to possess the virtues of both worlds. We have the opportunity. As older women and men, we can take seriously our mentoring role, act on the wisdom we've acquired, and use our experience for the common good. In addition, we can make room for younger people in our life; combat any signs of jaded, cynical attitude; ration our energy with care; and stay open to the reservoir of youthful energy in the world.

I'm one hour older than an hour ago. I look forward to the next hour.

"When I'm reading, when I'm really absorbed in a wonderful book, the sort of pleasure I feel is ageless—it occurs in a kind of dreamtime where the me who's reacting never changes. It's the only fountain of youth I've found."

~

One of the things that never changes, whether we're sixteen or sixty-three, is our completely free participation in the imaginative and fascinating world of books.

When we're young we discover the mysterious land of Oz with its Emerald City and yellow-brick road, life twenty thousand leagues under the sea, and we're able to accompany Alice to Wonderland. Once we've shared these experiences and others like them, we can never again be the same as we used to be before our discovery.

As a reader at eighty, we're the same literary adventurer-explorer as we were in junior high school. We turn the next page of an engrossing book with a long familiar aching anticipation of what is yet to come. Our eyes still grow wide in wonder.

Today, I'll find a new book and explore it as if it were a strange, compelling continent. I'm the same adventurer I always was.

"Ours seems to be an age of 'dirty tricks' in everything from sports to politics to money. Can someone try to live a normal, good life and avoid the pitfalls of the surrounding system?"

~

We hear so much about "making it" in our society. It's also called "winning" and "coming out on top."

But often we lose our soul in the act of establishing superiority. Oh yes, an end result may appear good in itself: winning an election or an athletic contest, making a successful business bid or commercial sale. What, however, was required of us?

Did an athlete use steroids in order to gain an edge over a competitor? Did a candidate use dirty tricks to pile up a bigger vote in an election? Did a developer endanger public health by concealing the existence of a toxic waste dump at a building site? The question also comes down to us. Are we willing to cheat or lie, exploit or cover up the facts, to gain an advantage? How much do we care about telling—and being told—the truth?

Today, I'll think about how I'm getting there, rather than where I'm going.

"In some other countries the older population is looked upon with respect and honor. I don't believe this is true in the United States."

~

Prejudice against older people is like prejudice against African Americans, Latinos, Asian Americans, Native Americans, women, gays and lesbians, handicapped people, and kids. It occurs when somebody seemingly feels a need to dislike or hate someone else, and finds an excuse by stereotyping.

Older women and men in the United States have many advantages, yet prejudice is often directed against them as a group. Some people seem to react angrily at the sight of white or gray hair, the very look of being older. Others object to older people moving slowly or driving a car more slowly. Possibly they are threatened by their own innate fear of growing older. Or they feel that older people stand in their way economically. Often they're rude.

Honor is accorded to few groups of people these days. Yet it is given to particular individuals who earn it. A high proportion of these are elderly people.

What is there in my life worthy of honor? I'll claim it.

"Many elderly people are prisoners in their own home to keep out of danger and trouble. You see, old people are fair game to knock around."

～

Predators represent danger to people who are particularly vulnerable, including children and older women and men.

It is foolish not to take every possible precaution for our safety. We need to lock the doors and windows of our home, avoid walking alone on a dark street and avoid carrying much money, know where we're going and how to get there, acquaint others with our comings and goings, take no chances, stay alert.

Having done all this, is there more that we should do? Yes. We cannot succumb to fear. We have a right to go out anytime we like. Although aware of danger, we must not let local Hitlers rule our lives or bully us. They must know we are not fair game to knock around. So, we have to be utterly sensible and not take obvious risks of any kind. A good rule is to be with others when we are outside. Watch carefully. Be firm.

I'll move carefully and sensibly through my world—but I won't be a prisoner.

"I am retired from a good job and if I ever feel lonely or depressed, I sit at my easel, pick up my paint brush, get out my paints, put some of the beauty I see on my canvas, and time begins to fly."

~

Blessed are those who know how to use their hands to make something useful or create a work of art.

Too many fret and stew, hour upon ghastly hour, not knowing how to entertain themselves or fill up the time in constructive ways. This happens whether they're alone or with others. But, if we're working with our hands, our solitariness or gregariousness becomes irrelevant. We're busy. We're doing something. Time seems to move along at a fast clip.

If we don't know how to use our hands, we can learn. Take a painting class or start one in sculpture or gardening or cooking or writing or playing an instrument. There are myriad things to learn how to do. We can take a closer look at activities engaged in by our friends and acquaintances. A whole new world of activity from a totally fresh perspective awaits us.

Today, I'll remember the pleasure I've taken in creating. I'll make the time to do it again.

"I'm a cute, feisty, li'l old lady with white hair who hasn't let her age and widowhood keep her down. I think other people perceive me as open-minded, flexible, friendly, fun, a little outrageous—and likable."

~

The difference between how others see us and how we see ourselves can be fascinating. When we think we're being generous, others might say we're overbearing with ego to burn. The same disparity extends to our appearance, work ability, spirituality, and how we get along with other people. Have you ever been shocked to see a photograph of yourself taken by someone else?

It's a good idea to build bridges between our self-evaluation—how we see ourselves—and how others see us. The wider the gap, the more we might be out of touch with our own reality. We can get significant pointers about ourself from people who are constantly around us. Maybe we've either evaded the truth or been unable to cope with it.

How do others perceive me? How close is that to the way I would be seen? Today, I'll think about how I can honestly make these one.

"It makes me sad to think of all those who died young and never got to know old age."

~

We've all known a wonderful young woman or man who died at an early age, and broke our heart by doing so. Departing so soon, this person seemed without an opportunity to fulfill a life of promise.

Yet who can clearly define life's promise? I believe it cannot be measured by years. Some people live more vividly and deeply within a brief but glorious period of time than others seem to do in a long but less eventful one.

The lesson to be learned is how to live as fully as possible within whatever span of years we have. It's tragic to ever put off living up to our finest potential. It's absurd to assume we'll have endless time. We can assume nothing at all about the amount of time we shall have. It is not a bad idea at all to live today as if it were our final one. Live it to the hilt.

The quality of life is far more important to me than the quantity.

"A fruit's ripening is natural and beneficial. It reminds me of aging."

~

Some older people are startlingly beautiful women and men. Their spiritual inner beauty is a revelation.

I think immediately of a couple whom I know. She is eighty-seven, he is eighty-three. It is one of life's rewards to be with them for a while. They are wiser than Socrates, have the liveliest sense of humor around, maintain a remarkably high level of interest in life, and convey a sense of joy in being together.

Such people are our best teachers on growing older. They show us how to resist a tendency to turn inward. Theirs is an example of how to embrace the world fondly, become interested in the lives of other people, listen intently, counsel patiently, and accept a mentoring role. The more we do this, the more others will want to come to us, share their thoughts and feelings, and be real friends. It means practicing unselfishness, appreciating life, pacing ourselves, and being truly interesting people whom others seek out.

How have I "ripened"? Today, I'll look for my wisdom, and share it.

"There are not enough hours in the day. I sew for my grand-kids. I have made a garden with cabbage, beets, squash, okra, corn, tomatoes, and beans. I am now canning."

∾

It is a blessing to be fully occupied in a way that satisfies and provides meaning for our life. Physical activity is great for us when it fits this scheme of things. We can see the results of our labor. What we do benefits other people who feel grateful as well as better for what we did.

A balance between activity and reflection is a good thing, too. Working in a garden can provide it. Whenever we're keeping very, very busy it's advisable to structure times when we can meditate. This lets us stand back from what we've been doing and see it within a larger perspective—our life. Meditation can sound scary and threatening to people: How deep within myself must I go? What if I get lost there? We need it because it's a way to bring balance into our life so that we can alternate between times of busyness and activity, on the other hand, and quiet reflection, on the other.

I promise myself some time close to the earth today. I'll work and reflect—and take strength.

"I kept wondering what to do with life. It seemed such a mystery. Then I decided to live."

~

We can look at our navel and ponder the mystery of life up to just a certain point. Then it's time to act.

Acting isn't hard because all the world's a stage and nearly everybody wants to do it. It's a great group exercise. Better than remaining passive and staying out of it forever. If life's a treat, enjoy it. Sure we might get burned, but what's wrong with a little fire?

Most of us commit to life. It's a lot different from navel gazing. The mystery of life loses a lot of its glamour when we're working our butt off for something we believe in. This can range from raising a family to working for civil rights, building a business to acquiring an education, composing music to taking self-improvement very seriously. We work and sweat, interact with others, and believe in something. Life is real, and we're living it.

Today I put aside the mystery—and live.

"As I regard it in my twilight years, the universe is a red bird that sits on a bough of a tree and looks at me."

~

There are numerous ways to regard the universe. One is to look through a telescope at Saturn and Mars. Another is to listen to a baby's heartbeat.

Many see the universe as out there somewhere. Others believe it lies within each of us. Where do we find the center of meaning? Perhaps in someone whom we love, our work or profession, or an unrealized dream. This becomes a highly personal matter. We find it difficult even to try putting it into words or explaining it to someone else.

Yet we do see the universe in our own special way. It's related to how we define life's meaning. It grows out of our life's roots and experiences. In the classic film *Citizen Kane* the single word *Rosebud* was found to encompass the mystery of a man's existence, his deepest feelings and motivations.

How do I see my universe? What would be my *Rosebud?* I'll look for the symbol of my own life today.

"Despite my years, I'm playing hardball with the sun; tennis with the moon. I'm having fun."

~

We make a big mistake in imbuing age with dignity and solidity when we leave out play and having a good time. Many men and women missed out on happiness earlier in life. They were forced to take on heavy responsibilities, sometimes to suffer emotional traumas. A delight of age is that it affords an opportunity to recapture lost joy.

Old age can mean cutting through a Gordian knot of stress and finding new outlets for expression and creativity. For many, the entire concept of self-realization and enjoyment was considered highly questionable when weighed against the seemingly unyielding demands of the work ethic. Yet this overlooked the richness and promise of our humanity. We have a constitutional right to the "pursuit of happiness" as a basic tenet of our national heritage. From a spiritual perspective, it is a much needed balance in our work-oriented lives.

I'll look for the source of joy in my life today.

"What staggers me is the shortness of life in comparison with all the things I want to do, places I want to see, people I want to meet."

∿

Life can seem short or long, depending on the circumstances.

We waste too much of life, especially when we're listless and bored instead of being energized and challenged. It's important to want to do lots of things and look forward to doing them. There is so much great music to hear, literature to read, cinema to see, food to eat. There are so many roses to smell, waterfalls to marvel at, oceans and lakes to swim in, hills and mountains to hike up. So many people to know, understand, experience, and learn from.

When we get tired, feel depressed, and wish to turn away from the world, it's a good idea to focus on something we can do instead. Make contact with someone. Help out where we're needed. Stay in touch with life.

Today, I'll turn my eyes from the calendar and clock, stop measuring—and live.

"I wonder how many people in the world have died in the last thirty seconds. How many were born? In comparison, how important is my own life?"

≈

Statistics can be staggering. I've watched an electric sign on a city building that reported every second the increases that took place in the world's population. It was hypnotizing.

We exist in earth's gigantic space that is filled with oceans, continents, mountains, and nations. Ulysses' journeys took years. Now people fly around the world in a few hours. Outer space offers yet another context. Looking up and staring at a star, it's easy to become overwhelmed by the sheer magnitude and complexity of the view.

We are here, too. At certain moments we feel a certain exhilaration that we are at the dead center of the whole universe. It seems, curiously, to be revolving about us, and our own problems and concerns momentarily block out everything else. Then, in a clearer moment, we realize how limited that view is. Instead we're a part of the cosmos, a vital and living part. Who we are, and what we do, is very important.

Looking at the sun, moon, planets, and stars, I feel a part of everything.

"I thought when I grew older I would come to golden years, but they are hard years."

∽

No years are perfect in themselves. There is no time in our life that is without problems or boasts only unyielding happiness.

As humans we tend to look forward to a desired state of perfection. Marriage will do it. Childbearing will provide it. Being in love will bring with it lasting perfection. The perfect job will resemble a mythical perfect wave. Creating a flawless work of art will usher in for us an experience of perfection.

On and on we go. The myth of golden years holds that we will bloom like roses in an ambience like Shangri-la, reinforced by wisdom and supported by others' unconditional love. But there is no such time. Always we continue to be faced with struggles, disappointment, losses, and ever new challenges. We can face each new day with fear and dread, or with courage, hope, and the best energy that we can muster. The choice is ours.

Today, I'll confront my struggles and losses unclouded by visions of Shangri-la.

"I wish I could stop talking about negative things and seeing everything as impossible, adding to my self-imposed misery."

~

We spend a disproportionate amount of time bitching about what is wrong in any given situation. Sure, something is wrong—always. But there's something right too.

A positive approach to living is to look for what's right as well as what's wrong. Then, to celebrate what is right, search out possibilities in it, and go to work and act upon them. Why do a number of people find evil more exciting than good? Evil conjures up lurid scenes out of hell. We tend to enjoy these as much as, say, a hot chocolate sundae with nuts and a cherry on top.

When the shouting is over, we're still here and life goes on as usual. We find that positive energy is a lot more helpful than negative. We need to accentuate the positive whenever we can. Give possibility a high priority over impossibility. Say that self-imposed misery is a drag. And stop it.

I don't have the time for misery.

"Remember, there are many friends in the public library. Books about travel, how-to, and every conceivable subject including people."

~

Some of our best friends are books. In many cases they're lifelong friends whom we have known intimately for many years. We got acquainted at the beginning of school and went on to share innumerable experiences under every possible kind of circumstance.

The public library is where they make their permanent home. We can roam the aisles between stacks, peruse titles and check authors' names, and choose from the widest range of themes and topics. Within a single hour we may come across adventure stories, histories of nations, suspense novels, biographies of presidents and poets, romance stories, cookbooks, autobiographies of renowned figures, collections of poems, bestsellers, and hidden treasures.

What riches await us. The public library is home for books that we love, so it is a home that awaits us, too.

I remember the last time I lost myself completely in a good book. I'll make the time to do that again.

"Envy is like a snake. It bit me. I need to get rid of the poison."

~

Envy is horrible. It transforms us from someone we know into a stranger. It can change us into a monster.

It's so unpredictable. Someone else receives honor, love, reward, and we go bonkers. Why? Envy is irrational. Suddenly we're confronted with someone else's well-being, and we can't stand it.

What is it that we want? What raises the shadow world into such a glaring distraction for us? Do we want the recipient of our envy to stub his or her toe? Or worse? We need to place the situation in perspective and try to be rational about our feelings. For starters, let's recognize the extraordinary diversity in all our lives. As people, we're very different. Some of us are successful in this way, others in that way. There's plenty of room for both. Envy is a warning. We need to find out why someone else's recognition or success bothers us so much.

Today I'm going to imagine my life empty of envy. What if I were happy with the life I've made?

"It is vital for us not so much to expect a miracle each day, but to accept the miracles as they are brought to us."

≈

Our daily expectations need to be brought into balance with what life gives us. We can be decidedly unhappy if we have deep wishes out of sync with our possibilities and skills.

Let's try to make peace with life. Every day represents a miracle that we're here. A number of smaller miracles also come our way. These include acts of kindness, love, friendship, sustenance, and new possibilities that surprise us.

What can we do with the miracles? I suppose we can just take them for granted, dismiss them from our conscious thought, and treat them as if they were mundane and unneeded interlopers. Of course, an alternative is to feel gratitude for them as wonderful gifts that embolden and magnify our lives. Acceptance implies our openness to the miracle, when our empty hands are outstretched and filled.

Today I make peace with life. I'll be realistic about my wishes and demands. I'll welcome any miracles.

"Cling onto any shred of better things to come. The best I can offer to anybody having difficulties is not to give up on hope."

~

There are isolated moments in our human life that seem to resemble hell. The bottom drops out. We are transfixed by pain, left stark naked by failure, embarrassed beyond our capacity to take it.

At such a moments we feel powerless. There seems little or nothing to hold onto. We have been stripped of pride. Nothing makes sense. This is precisely when we need to know there is something to hold onto, something to make sense. And there is. We've just got to find it or let it find us. This is a moment when our life can be saved. Wiser than before, we can go on living. We can pick up the pieces and start over.

Hope is our way to survive. It is the lifeline. A remarkable thing about hope is that we can bear it to each other. We are able to carry the lifeline to someone else, or receive it in a moment when it saves us.

When I'm sinking, I'll look for a lifeline. I'll find it when I need it.

"Different parts of me are charging off in various directions today. I want unity of purpose in my life."

≈

Each of us has a number of different people under our skin, trying to get ahead, occupy center stage, work and play.

It's up to us to relate kindly to the cast of characters under our skin. There are radicals and conservatives, romantic figures and very sober ones, lazy laid-back funsters and hard-driving, ambitious go-getters. It requires all our wisdom, perseverance, and loving to relate to this mix of people. We don't like certain parts of ourself as much as others. Some even embarrass us and we try to disown them. This inevitably backfires because all these parts constitute us. They're who we are.

If we want unity of purpose in our life, we have to grant the different people under our skin equal time. Attempt to meet their demands, but make them realize they can't be relentlessly selfish. They need to realize that they are parts of our wholeness.

I resolve to make getting along with myself a full-time job.

"They once said not to trust anybody over thirty or forty. What has age to do with trust? Wouldn't someone older be more trustworthy?"

~

Deciding whom we may trust is a tricky business. We are looking for people who have ideals, a sense of inherent goodness, a strong honest streak, and a touch of unselfishness.

Young or old may fill the bill. It isn't a question of age. It concerns individual commitment. There is a view, however, that corruption grows with age; so do selfishness and cynical adaptation to the status quo. Nonsense! Balderdash!

There are hucksters, egomaniacs, manipulators, exploiters, and sellouts both young and old. We find as many older men and women who fight for justice as young ones; as many young men and women who struggle for needed social change as old ones. The big question is: How trustworthy do we manage to be?

Whom do I trust in my life? What is it about them that inspires belief? I'm going to look for those qualities, and cultivate them in my own life.

"I remember someone said we're all spectators of our own lives. What does that mean?"

～

The best show in town is people. We observe the conduct and actions of others constantly, especially movie and sports stars, bona fide royalty, and politicians.

We keep track of our own lives best. There is more than a bit of narcissism in all of us. We catch quick glances of ourselves in mirrors at unsuspecting moments, gaze at full-length images of ourselves in reflecting shop windows while we walk on the street.

What do we think when we see ourselves so candidly? The truth is that we have already created our own public images for others to see. So our image may reflect strong extroversion even if we're shy, sophistication even if we're untutored and simple, generosity even if we have a natural Scrooge-like nature. We do put our best foot forward. This is all right if we maintain a sense of humor about it, know what we're doing, and never lose contact with who we really are.

Today, I'll explore who I really am instead of who I'm supposed to be.

"Can I learn how to grow old? If so, who can teach me?"

~

We have to be able to live as fully as possible at each stage of our life. When we're growing up, peers are our best teachers. We learn from each other.

Growing older, role models become increasingly important. We observe people who have managed to age with charm, care, and wisdom, and other people admire and love them.

Finally, it comes down to ourselves. Why not? We've had a lifetime to learn. We know a lot more than we started out. We've been burned on occasion, felt the sting of adversity and the whip of cruelty, sunk into the morass of failure. Not only do we know about life but also about ourselves—the games we play, our strengths and weaknesses, the ruses we are adept at, and the sense of meaning that can be found at the deepest part of us. We can become our own best teachers about how to grow old.

I resolve to learn one new thing every day.

"I want to commune quietly with life instead of using it as a racetrack."

≈

It's up to each of us, to a great extent, how we choose to treat life. We can be gentle or fierce, hating or loving, cold or warm, accepting or rejecting. We can also work out our own combinations of these.

A combination may be our wisest choice. For example, we may not have enough control over the elements in our life to be able either to commune quietly alone or to move quickly in the fast race. Instead, a smattering of each might be necessary for us. We can learn how to meditate quietly at certain moments and, at the same time, be involved in the action of life.

Living is an art. It requires sensitivity as well as commitment, tender awareness along with strong zeal. Most of us cannot go off by ourselves to live in a quiet outpost of the global village. However, we can often both define and determine the quality of life that we want.

Today, I'll find a point of quiet and stay there for a while.

"Whether we're old or young, we're all together in a jet plane called life. We might as well try to enjoy the trip."

～

The mix of people in our common life is amazing. Someone is always being born while someone else is about to enter high school; yet others just got married, started a promising new job, retired from work, or are holding a new grandchild.

We're all in life together. Older people need to remember what it was like to be young. How it felt to fall in love for the first time. How much courage it took to go out on that initial job hunt. How painful was that awful sense of failure when the whole world seemed about to collapse.

Younger people need to see older ones as people not statistics standing in their way or stereotypes that are objects of ridicule. Young women and men need to find role models of aging and mentors among their older friends—people whom they genuinely admire for their perseverance, and respect for their contributions to life. Human experience is incredibly similar, and neither youth nor age changes it essentially.

I won't let the expectations of my age color my reactions to life. I'll respond from the core of my being.

"I'm older and more mature, but I still take myself too seriously."

∼

It's a fine balance that we must sustain between not taking ourselves seriously enough and taking ourselves too seriously.

We deny ourselves essential dignity when we refuse to treat our life with respect and love. Our life is a wonderful and incredible gift. To throw it on a dump heap of abuse or indifference is to deny its worth. We cannot let other denigrate our life, either. Our attitude of reverence for all of life, including our own, is a means of survival.

We'll always wish to balance dignity with humor and humility. We are aware that life's a stage. Surely we know that our performance doesn't always deserve rave reviews. This makes us the same as other people. Let's share center stage graciously with them. Applause and boos will be equally shared, too. Hopefully, we'll be able to smile at the whole show.

Do I take myself too seriously? Today, I'll aim for honesty and humility in presenting myself to others.

"We need to learn how not to cry over spilled milk."

~

What's done is done. We can't recall angry words we just uttered, and clearly regret. We can't erase the past five years from our consciousness.

Granted. Yet it's futile to play a bad scene over and over again in our mind. To wallow in anguish. To feel a martyr or a villain in dozens of reruns of a life scene. Doing it drains our energy. It can inflict permanent damage on our close relationships.

The best thing to do with spilled milk is get a rag or sponge and clean it up. Quickly. But to say it isn't there is both silly and impossible. It is there. Having cleaned it up, our next task is to see what effects the spill had. Did it have any effect on us? On other people? Was there a reason milk got spilled? What was it? Let's try to understand what happened. Talk about it. What's done is done, but, like a pebble in a lake, it can cause ripples for a long time to come.

Today, I'll resolve an old conflict. My reward will be the relief of a clean slate.

"At seventy-seven I enjoy the computer my children gave me for my seventy-fifth birthday, write a poem now and then, correspond with old friends, play the piano at home and in two nursing homes, and enjoy my life to the best of my ability."

∼

To enjoy life to the best of our ability is a secret of living at any age. The key words here are *enjoy* and *ability*. It takes a certain ability to enjoy. Far too many people, sadly, do not enjoy life much at all. When this occurs, something is seriously the matter. We're meant to enjoy life. Savor it. Appreciate it.

Our enjoyment of life needs to be based less on what we're supposed to enjoy than what we do enjoy. We can't follow an etiquette book here. Moral platitudes are out of place. It's just us, here, and reality, there—with nothing in between. If we've been behaving like robots all these years, pretending to enjoy what others thought we should, it's clearly time to find out the truth. Other people's opinions don't matter nearly as much as our own.

Where is the pleasure in my life? It's what keeps me alive. I'll make time for more.

"*Don't ever tell this gal that peace does not exist! I found strength in peace after battling alcoholism for years, and weakness most of my life.*"

∽

Isn't peace wonderful? It isn't far away at all. It's here. We can share it.

Imprisonment within fear, hatred, or substance abuse is a killer. Many of us know it well. Daily battle with it is a hard story, with many ups and downs, defeats and victories. Always, the judgments and pains of others are involved, too.

Weakness is something we all share in one form or another. No one is strong without it. However, our weakness needs to be turned into strength. How can we do it? By working at it, refusing to give up, and seeking help when we need it instead of proudly trying to rely on our own resources. To get well requires support, networking, honesty, self-examination without flinching, and a vision of health and wholeness. Such a vision at our darkest hour can serve as the hinge of the door. The door is peace. We can walk through the door. It is open.

Peace may be close at hand, among my friends and ordinary surroundings. I'll claim it.

"*Everyone is born with a creative spirit. Creating something can range from cutting out paper dolls to composing a great piece of music.*"

~

Creation is wonderful, isn't it? It takes many forms. Its impulse is life's energy. Creation keeps us alive, seeking ever new ways of expression.

One of the best things about creative energy is that we want to share with others what we have created. It's no fun sitting alone in a room surrounded by one's paintings, sketches, or sculpture. We want to invite others to see it, too. We need their criticism. It's important for us to know how others relate to our work and what meaning they find in it.

Some of us play a musical instrument or sing, others dance or compose music. Some write poems, essays, or stories, while others speak lines. Always we should encourage other people to discover the sources of their own creative energy. We need them to help us discover our own. Creation isn't selfish. It means sharing.

When did I last make something totally new? When did I have the satisfaction of creating something from nothing? Today, I'll flex my talents—for others, for me.

"Most of us seniors are sharp as a tack and can run circles around eighteen-year-olds who think they're ultrasmart when actually they are wet behind the ears."

~

I find human beings are miracles. They amaze me. I love the wisdom and maturity of age, and also the drive and spunk of youth. There is, thank God, room for both.

Some seniors, I must say, are not sharp as a tack, while some youth cannot be described as wet behind the ears. Generalities are not helpful here. What matters is being able to see each other as we are. This includes perceiving the gifts and skills, the faults and limitations of each.

Ironically, there are some seniors who are characterized by spunk and drive instead of maturity and wisdom. At the same time, some youths are in fact old souls. Their wisdom and maturity are known to all in their family and school settings. If they lack anything, it's spunk and drive. The solution? Let's try for well-rounded lives seasoned by all the good spices we can get.

I'm full of spunk and wisdom. I'll strive to balance them.

"Realization dawned on me that no one else is going to solve my problems. I have to. Underneath years of unhappiness I discovered myself as a new person whose life is worthwhile."

∾

One of the worst exercises in futility is to wait for someone else to come along like Galahad and rescue us while we languish in frustration and weakness, feel victimized, and lack the courage or strength to make a decision.

Yet we must. The beginning of wisdom is the realization that no one else can do this for us. When we refuse to realize it, we remain indecisive, looking perpetually to left and right, but not moving forward. This creates great unhappiness not only for ourselves, but also for other people who are connected to our lives, and can lead to extremely serious problems at home, in our relationships, at work, within our minds and souls; and beyond these, in our expectations or sense of failure, or use of money, and the very direction our lives are taking.

Self-discovery as a worthwhile person is an extremely positive experience. A key is required, however. The key is our individual initiative. This grows out of our awareness that no one else can live our life for us.

Today, I'll take the wheel. I'll try taking responsibility for my own life. I'll set out to discover where that may lead.

"*If people allow themselves a chance to get involved in something other than their disappointments, they can loosen the death grip they keep on their agony.*"

~

Who wants agony? Probably none of us. Yet a number of us remain locked inside it.

Disappointments can multiply, especially if we're counting. They seem to feed on one another. Then we get to a place where we expect to be disappointed. This sets in motion a lot of negative energy. The best solution is to focus on the opposite of disappointment: new changes, new opportunities. They exist. We block their view, especially if our focus does not include their possibility. If we have already decided we're going to be disappointed again—again and again—we make it virtually impossible for fresh ideas to come into our line of vision, let alone be dealt with in positive ways.

Try to realize: Life is life—we're alive! Life always means anything can happen to us, including the unexpected, good, and even revolutionary things.

Today I'll try exerting positive energy in every aspect of my life. I'll meet the world anew.

"If I knew that I had just five months to live, what would I want to do?"

≈

It is a classic question for all of us. Some would choose travel to places they had always yearned to visit. Others might stay home and get life's affairs in order, or finish a significant piece of creative work, maybe meditate in a quiet place and go fishing.

Most of us would probably want to appreciate life for the last time—savor its richness, honor its simplicity, marvel at its intricate complexity. We'd have reached a precious moment to hear a favorite selection of music for the last time, read a beloved poem or book, dine on a cherished dish, or swim off a treasured beach.

Yet we can do these things now. We don't have to wait until we have just five months to live.

What would I do today if it were my last? I'll try living each day that way.

"How can I deal honestly with my life as it is, not as I wish it were?"

~

The best way? Open our eyes wide, look around and see what's there, take a deep breath, and dive decisively into the center of life as if it were a deep pool of water.

Simple? Yes and no. Unquestionably, it can be done. But many people refuse. You see, it requires giving up mere wishing. It demands that we acknowledge what is clearly before our very eyes.

Growing older, we are foolish to choose dishonesty over honesty about life. Now our decisions take on a literal survival meaning. They can define the remainder of our life on earth and also our eternal goals of the spirit. They are extraordinarily powerful. We hold this power in our hands.

I'm going to look life squarely in the eye.

"I keep asking myself if I have anything left to strive for."

∽

It is so easy to give up. It can become a long, drawn-out process of denying hope and elevating low self-esteem to an art.

We should never measure ourselves against the world's images of success. In fact, much imagery of that kind is sheer fabrication. The world's greatest movie star may be an emotional disaster while an unknown clerk is an enormous success at the business of living. Each of us is unique, possessing creation's inner beauty and a startling capacity for life.

What is left to strive for? Here are a few things. Love in a world filled with too much hatred. Honesty in small things as well as big ones. Justice in human situations that flagrantly deny it. Joy in place of despair. Courage to change what needs to be changed. Laughter to ease pain. Beauty to illuminate the soul. Compassion to outlaw cruelty. Patience to survive with grace. It's clear that all of us need to strive all the time for what is better, brighter, and lifts up life to its full potential.

I'll look for things to awaken my soul. I'll see the wonder of living.

"I try to giggle thirteen times a day. Sounds hard but gradually it becomes so foolish, it's fun. Cost? None."

~

We need to bring fun into life. Just simple, ridiculous, belly-laughing fun. Are we afraid of fun? Does it embarrass us? Maybe it seems foolishly childish to us very, very serious grown-ups! How many years have we struggled to keep a straight face?

Giggling thirteen times a day might be a good start. We could follow that by learning how to laugh at pomposity, howl at phoniness. Potential scenarios are limitless.

A great gift as we grow older is to become mellower, laugh more gently and often, and gaze openly at the emperor parading without clothes. It's been said that in the divine comedy, God must have a wonderful sense of humor. Why? Because God created us.

With all of life's manifold struggles and problems, it behooves us to practice the art of laughter. Let's have fun. Let's place things in perspective and never be afraid of looking foolish.

I'm going to enjoy what's ridiculous and not let anyone ever take it away from me.

"I realize trying to hold tight control of my life is impossible and stupid—but it's so hard to let go."

∾

It's also hard not to let go. Which do we want? The difficulty of the task is not the issue. The real question is: Which is best? Which is more realistic?

It's true that the more we let go of control and rigidity, the better our physical health is apt to be, the better our mental health will be, and the better our spiritual health will be. And the better our relationship to life and the planet will be.

It's not terribly hard to let go. Sure, it will be difficult if we succumb to doom-like fears, tighten our bodies to the breaking point, shoot up our blood pressure, and treat the entire project as it were World War III. The secret is to let go by letting go. It falls into place. There's a bonus. We've managed to relinquish an element of our life that blocked us, creating harm and alarm.

Today, I'll drop the reins for a while. I'll find out where my life wants to go.

"*To fill a void in my life I decided to pursue an old dream. I looked for something I'd always loved and wanted to do, but never attempted.*"

~

We needn't always concentrate on having a new dream. An old dream may be especially informative, once we've dreamed it a long time.

There are special things all of us have wanted to do, but the moment for them never came. These may range from learning a foreign language to writing poems, from playing a cello to doing volunteer work with disenfranchised kids, from becoming a priest to taking up archery, from dancing to joining a cooking school, from completing a long-abandoned degree to taking up painting.

A big question is: What did we never attempt that interested us? It might be climbing Mt. Everest but could also include performance art at a nearby community college, writing one's life story for children in the family, planting an herb garden, or rising very, very early to watch birds.

Today, I'll dream an old dream. Then I'll make it real.

"I find that the habit of despair is a bottomless pit. I wonder if I can achieve the habit of hope instead?"

∽

Hope is always possible—but a change in focus is necessary. If we stare into a bottomless pit of despair, we cannot at the same time be looking with anticipation into the bright face of hope.

Sometimes we need to look away from the bottomless pit of despair. This requires an act of will or at least our being open to distraction. Even a firecracker exploding can provide a moment's release from the absorption of staring into a bottomless pit. A moment's release is all that is required.

A change of focus is one of the great gifts of life. In a moment's flash, we can gain a new view, a fresh perspective, an actual change. Something, or everything, suddenly looks different. Where there was absolute hopelessness, now there is absolute possibility. We have all experienced this, but not often enough. We should make it a habit to change focus.

Today, I'll look at my life in a new way. Where there is hope, I will find it.

ABOUT THE AUTHOR

Malcolm Boyd is the best-selling author of twenty-nine books. Among them, *Are You Running With Me Jesus?*, *As I Live and Breathe: Stages of an Autobiography*, *Free to Live, Free to Die*, *Christian: Its Meaning in an Age of Future Shock*, *A Malcolm Boyd Reader*, and *Samuel Joseph for President*.

The New York Times Book Review describes his work as "provocative, witty, and highly entertaining." *The Christian Century* says, "Boyd is a prophet for our times."

A three-term president of PEN Center USA West, and an Episcopal priest for more than fifty years, Boyd spent his formative years in Hollywood where he was the Production Partner of Mary Pickford in PRB, Inc., and President of the Television Producers Association of Hollywood.

In 2005, Boyd received the prestigious Unitas Award from Union Theological Seminary in New York City. The citation read: "Poet, priest, pioneer; for his activism in the Civil Right movement; for his lasting influence as a role model for gay clergy; and for his best selling spiritual classic, *Are You Running with Me, Jesus?*"

The author resides in California with his life partner, author, artist, and activist, Mark Thompson. Read more about Malcolm Boyd at www.malcolmboyd.com

5957945R0

Made in the USA
Lexington, KY
02 July 2010